Sunset BARBECUE COOK BOOK

Sunset

BARBECUE

BY THE EDITORS OF SUNSET BOOKS

AND SUNSET MAGAZINE

Lane Books · Menlo

COOK BOOK

ILLUSTRATIONS BY
CAROL JOHNSTON

Park, California

FOREWORD

This book is intended to provide the barbecue chef, both novice and expert, with the necessary technical information and tested recipes to make barbecuing easy and successful. The technical information includes tips on firemanship and the use of various types of barbecues and equipment. Every recipe has been prepared and tested by the home economics department of *Sunset Magazine*.

The index is specifically designed to help you quickly find a suitable recipe for any occasion. As in other cook books, the recipes are indexed by name and type of meat or ingredients. A special feature of this index is the listing of recipes by the method of barbecuing. If you want to use a rotary spit for example, turn to Spit-Roasting in the index: All the recipes for spit-roasting are listed by the type of meat.

The editors would like to express their thanks to Lloyd Bryan and W. A. Leak, who contributed expert know-how in the fine art of barbecue cookery.

COVER PHOTOGRAPH By ROBERT COX

Ninth Printing March 1975

CONTENTS

BARBECUE TECHNIQUES 6

COOKING on SKEWERS 20

BEEF 26

LAMB 44

PORK 50

VARIETY MEATS 56

GAME 60

POULTRY 62

FISH and SHELLFISH 72

SAUCES and MARINADES . . 80

SIDE DISHES 86

INDEX 92

BARBECUE TECHNIQUES

Barbecuing is one of the easiest ways to entertain as well as one of the most enjoyable. The following chapter discusses various barbecue techniques and equipment that will help you, as a beginner or a seasoned chef, to achieve consistent success.

BARBECUE EQUIPMENT

You don't need complicated equipment for good barbecue cooking. All over the world, hungry people have devised methods to cook their meat or fish over an open wood fire with whatever implements they had on hand.

Probably the oldest of these simple techniques is to skewer meat on a stick, the principle of the hot dog roast or the Arab shish kebab. When the food is too heavy to hold or suspend, an alternate to skewers is to place the food on a grill or on open coals.

The basic principles remain valid. Whether the equipment you use is plain or fancy, some kind of barbecue stove is advisable in our era of patios, gardens, and apartment balconies.

Small Portable Barbecues

Tiny portable barbecues answer several special needs—indoor, table-top cooking of appetizers, or the cooking of a meal for two.

If you like a traditional approach, you may prefer the heavy metal hibachis or the ceramic Mexican braseros. With just a few coals you can grill skewered meats and seafood for a small family or turn out enough appetizers for a few friends. When you have too many people to do the cooking directly on the grill, the hibachis or braseros can be used as an attractive heat source for warming appetizers and skewers cooked elsewhere.

The Mexican braseros come in terra cotta or in hard-fired black Oaxacan pottery. Too hot a fire can crack or break either kind. It's best to build a fire of no more than

ten briquets to begin with, then slowly add more when the pottery is hot. The fire goes into the upper bowl, while the large, lower, decorated bowl is a draft chamber. Frequently, braseros are not sold with grills, so you have to buy one separately to fit the firebowl.

More modern versions of the table-top barbecue have such features as adjustable grills, wind screens, shish-kebab holders, and even rotisseries. Many of them are just scaled-down versions of standard barbecues, while others resemble suitcases, frying pans, or buckets. There are even electric models that use no charcoal at all.

A few of these tiny barbecues are quite specialized. On one your only fuel is newspaper; on another you can smoke cook; still others are specifically designed for hamburgers or hot dogs for picnic outings.

The Versatile Brazier

The next step up in size and complexity is the bowl-shaped brazier barbecue with three or four legs and two wheels for easy transport. At their simplest, braziers are just shallow metal bowls with a grid on top. They are adequate for barbecuing hamburgers, steaks, pieces of poultry, or fish. For more control over your cooking, or for larger pieces of food, you can equip braziers with adjustable grills, wind screens, half hoods, and rotisseries. To do roasts on the grill, or for smoke cooking, you can make a foil dome to fit the entire brazier bowl (instructions given on page 14), or enclose a half-hood with foil.

Most such braziers come apart for winter storage or for carrying to a picnic site or campground.

Covered Barbecues

A covered barbecue with dampers to control fire temperature makes cooking large pieces of food much easier and more economical. Since you have such efficient control over the heat, even on windy or wet days, the covered barbecue is like a kitchen outdoors combining a broiler, oven, smoker, and grill.

The simplest covered barbecue is the kettle-shaped model. The deep fire bowl has a bottom damper, and the dome lid has a second damper. When you put a roast on the grill and cover it, the reflected heat in the dome browns the top as oven heat would do. If it cooks too fast, just close the dampers a bit to lower the heat. If there's still good charcoal left when your food is done, close both bottom and top dampers to snuff it out and you can relight it the next time.

Another variation on the covered barbecue is the cylinder or rectangular box mounted on a wagon. Some can be purchased without the wagon for permanent installation.

Both the cylinder and box often include an air temperature thermometer in the lid, so there's no guesswork involved in adjusting heat. You can also adjust the distance between food and coals by either raising the grill or lowering the fire grate. Some models have a fire door which allows you to add or rearrange coals without opening the top and letting the heat escape. There are usually dampers bottom and top for further heat control.

If you buy one of these large and expensive wagon barbecues, look for one made of heavy metal with a finish that won't be damaged by heat. Some include grill racks that slope toward a drip trough so that fat doesn't go into the fire. A few of them have a built-in electric coil to start the charcoal.

Many accessories are available for the wagon barbecues. Depending on the model, you can buy rotisseries, smoking equipment, special Dutch ovens, extra grills, and shish-kebab cookers.

The barrel or egg-shaped covered barbecue is influenced by a Japanese smoke oven called the kamado. It is the most specialized and least adapted to ordinary grilling, although you can grill if you wish. It is probably the most economical for long cooking, since a small amount of charcoal can be damped to burn slowly for hours.

The kamado has a damper near ground level and a chimney with lid or sliding door at the top. Inside, a ceramic bowl holds charcoal, and a cylindrical sleeve holds the grill well above it. The bowl is intended to hold only 20 or 30 briquets or the equivalent amount of plain charcoal, and heat is controlled exclusively by the dampers. You light the charcoal with both dampers wide open, then shut them almost entirely for long cooking or for smoking. Since it is difficult to add more fuel (the charcoal is entirely enclosed when the grill is in place) you should start with the fire bowl filled to capacity. If coals are left at the end of the cooking time they snuff themselves out when the dampers are closed.

Gas and Electric Units

Traditionalists may stop reading here, since the idea of gas or electric barbecues without charcoal may make them gnash their teeth, but these units are becoming very popular and do give a definite barbecue flavor to the foods cooked on them. In addition, they are more economical to use than charcoal barbecues, and they heat ready to use in just a few minutes. Cleaning is no problem either, since no ash is produced and drips burn away rather quickly.

Although cooking techniques are about the same with gas or electric units, the initial adjustment is critical with gas. Be sure when your unit is installed that the lowest setting produces about 300° of heat with the top down. Your only control is the gas cock, since there are no coals to remove.

All gas barbecues and many electric ones use fuel to heat ceramic or volcanic rock "coals" which then supply radiant energy to cook the food above them. Fat drips onto these coals and flares or smokes to produce a barbecued look and flavor. For stronger smoke flavor, you can sprinkle hickory chips over the coals.

Some electric units do away with the ceramic or rock entirely and use only an electric coil under a heavy metal grill. With these there is still somewhat of a barbecue flavor and a most pleasing appearance, since the grill heats enough to sear strips across the meat. These units are only for grilling or spit roasting.

Gas barbecues may be permanently installed, using natural gas, or they may be portable, using a tank of LP gas. Either way they ignite immediately and heat their ceramic or rock elements in about ten minutes. On units using chunks of volcanic rock to radiate heat, the rock can become discolored by dripping fat. If you want to clean it, just turn it over with the dark side toward the gas burner. The intense heat burns it white as you cook.

Both gas and electricity are excellent for indoor barbecues since they require less powerful ventilating systems

than you need for the dangerous fumes of burning charcoal. Electric units require a 220-volt line, as do other major electrical appliances, but can be installed in a protected permanent barbecue area outdoors provided they aren't exposed to the wear and tear of the elements.

ACCESSORIES

You can equip yourself with mountains of barbecue accessories, some of which are very useful, while others are just amusing gimmicks.

The Basics

First of all you'll need something to light the fire. Once the fire is going, other accessories will depend upon the type of meat and the method of barbecuing you are using. Here are the most common implements:

Tongs: A long pair of tongs with good gripping ends are used for fire arranging. If you're of the don't-pierce-the-meat school, tongs can be used to turn the meat.

Brushes: A stiff metal brush, with or without a scraper, keeps your grill free of burned particles.

Spatulas and Forks: Long handled forks and spatulas help turn the sputtering meat.

Mitts: Mitts are useful for handling hot metal; a good cotton apron helps keep you presentable.

Thermometers: Covered units often have built-in thermometers. You can tell the temperature at a glance all through the cooking periods and can add or arrange coals as soon as necessary.

A meat thermometer for large cuts of meat tells you just exactly how done the meat is. This is even more important in barbecuing than in oven cooking, since time is much more variable and dependent on distance from the heat, the wind, and the weather.

Knives: Get the best carving knife available, and always use it with a carving board. Have it sharpened by an expert a couple times a year. (A good knife shouldn't require sharpening more often than this, but you can hone it before use to even up any tiny nicks and roughness.)

Skewers: Buy some long skewers for shish kebab. Wooden handles are nice, but your mitt will protect you if you decide on the more practical metal rods. In any event, really long skewers can be placed with the grip well away from the fire so they won't heat up too much. You can also buy a rotary shish-kebab attachment that holds and turns six or eight skewers. These look dramatic and, most important, save you the trouble of hand-turning the skewers.

Spit-Roasting Gear

True spit roasting is one of the prime joys of barbecuing. You can find spit assemblies for even small portable barbecues.

The basics of spit roasting consist of a strong motor to turn large roasts and poultry without laboring, a spit that shows no tendency to bend, and a pair of spit forks to hold food in place as it turns. Basic accessories to consider are:

Extra Spit Forks: Extra forks are convenient for holding rows of small poultry solidly.

Balance Weights: With a balance weight you can adjust the center of gravity while the food is cooking so that it turns evenly. One kind of weight slips over the spit and screws down. Point it toward the lighter side of a poorly balanced roast. The weight is adjustable toward or away from the spit. If there are changes in balance, shift the weight toward the spit to make it lighter, pull it away to make it heavier.

Pliers: Pliers are useful to tighten screws on spit forks.

PREPARING THE FIREBED

Before stoking the charcoal, many barbecue chefs like to line the firebed with foil, or with sand or gravel. The foil, shiny side up, makes cleaning easier and reflects a certain amount of extra heat. Sand or gravel protects the metal of the firebed from overheating; gravel supplies a certain amount of bottom draft and is particularly good with a light metal and solid-bottomed barbecue.

Sand or foil liners can simply be discarded every few weeks when you clean out the barbecue. If you want to

save gravel for reuse when it gets really greasy, pour it into a bucket of warm detergent suds; then dry it thoroughly before lighting a fire on it. Wet gravel sometimes pops when heated.

Don't bother to clean the firebed too often. A layer of ash or some grease won't impede your cooking.

Fuel

Charcoal briquets are quick and, being uniform in size, easy to arrange under the grill.

Briquets vary widely in their composition, but the material used to form them is indicated somewhere on the sack. Most seasoned barbecue cooks prefer briquets with a hardwood or fruit-pit base, although other materials, including anthracite coal, are sometimes used. Whatever the base, the material is first converted into charcoal, then ground, mixed with a binder, and pressed into shape. Each kind burns a little differently than the others, so cooking heats and times depend strongly on the kind of briquet you use. Once you've discovered how long it takes to prepare coals and cook your favorite recipe with one brand, you'll probably prefer to stick to it. In particular, don't try a new brand when guests are coming.

You can still use hardwood — oak, fruit wood — for a large-scale pit barbecue, but you will have a long wait for cord wood to become glowing coals. Never use soft wood such as pine. It burns hot, gives off resinous smoke, and won't develop adequate coals.

Starting the Fire

Charcoal briquets can be hard to light. If you already have a favorite method there's no reason to change, but if you're new to outdoor cooking, or not very proficient at fire starting, here are a few ways, old and new, that will enable you to produce glowing embers in the shortest

You don't need too many coals. Charcoal fires are hot, and for grilling under normal circumstances, 25 to 30 coals should be adequate. For roasting thick pieces of meat or whole birds you may have to add more coals in the course of cooking. Allow 15 minutes for them to ignite at the edges of the fire. The more open the barbecue, the more coals you need, since the heat escapes and the charcoal burns more quickly.

Arranging the Coals

When you grill, arrange the coals to cover the entire area under the food. If the fire seems too hot, and the coals flame up because of dripping fat, space them farther apart with tongs, making a checkerboard pattern of coals and empty spaces. If there are still occasional flareups, keep a water pistol or spray bottle on hand and lightly douse the flaming coals. If the coals are easy to reach, you can drop a lettuce leaf over the flame. It quickly burns to ash.

Don't cook over coals that are not completely covered with ash. Coals that are still spotted with black or are flaming a good deal are much more likely to flare and smoke, and the heat they produce is uneven. It's not flame that cooks barbecued foods, but direct infra-red radiation that comes from completely heated coals.

When you add coals while cooking, place them at the edge of the fire, well away from the food. The smoke won't smudge your dinner, and they'll be ready in 15 minutes.

You can develop excellent flavor in food by burning something aromatic in the coals, even when your barbecue is not covered. Hickory chips are the most used flavor additive. Put them on either early or late in the cooking, or keep a few going all the time if you're smoke cooking. A few garlic buds in the fire toward the end of the cooking period add pungency. If there's thyme or rosemary in the garden, or a few bay leaves on hand, throw them on in the last few minutes for a special aroma. Twigs of fruit wood also add aroma and flavor.

GRILL COOKING

Straight grill cooking is useful for quickly cooked foods such as steaks, chops, ground meat patties, sausages, small fish, and poultry parts. And skewered foods cook just as well right on a grill as they do on special rotating attachments. With a little ingenuity, you can adapt a grill to cook larger pieces of food, either by covering the whole thing with a foil dome, or by placing a tent of foil directly over the food (directions for making a foil dome are given on page 14).

possible time. Whatever method you choose, allow 30 to 45 minutes between lighting up and cooking.

Electric Starters: Many versions of the electric starter are available, and some barbecues have them built in. You place the resistance coil of the simplest kind in the firebed, pour coals over it, plug it in, and the coals are ready for cooking in 20 to 30 minutes.

Chimney Starters: A fire chimney, either home-made or bought, creates a strong draft through the coals and decreases the time necessary to ignite them. The simplest version is a two or three-pound coffee can with top and bottom removed. Punch holes around the bottom edge. Place two wadded sheets of newspaper or marinated coals in the bottom, fill the chimney with briquets, and light. You'll have coals ready for cooking in 20 to 30 minutes. Just remove the chimney and begin.

Inflammable Liquids and Jelly: A number of these are sold specifically for lighting charcoal. (The liquids are petroleum products for which you can substitute paint thinner. The jelly is jellied alcohol like that used for canned heat.)

With the liquids, either douse a pyramid of coals, wait a minute for the liquid to soak in, then light, or place several briquets in a closed can or wide-mouthed jar and cover them with fluid, allowing it to soak in until the briquets stop bubbling. You can keep "marinated" briquets on hand all the time, ready for barbecuing at short notice. Just place two or three at the bottom of the briquet pyramid, cover them up, and light. Using this method of dousing or marinating with a pyramid of 25 briquets, you should have coals ready for cooking in 30 to 40 minutes.

With the jelly, you again prepare a pyramid, then push two or three spoonfuls of jelly into the crevices. Be sure it's well under the briquets or you may not get a good start. If you position it properly, you will have cooking coals in 30 to 40 minutes.

Directions for preparing and arranging a fire for grill cooking appear in the section under firemanship on page 10. Before placing food on a new or freshly cleaned grill, rub the grill with a piece of fat or a little oil so food won't stick to the hot grid. Don't bother to clean the grid after each barbecue. Each time, wait until it is heated by the fire, then scrape and brush it with a metal brush. You remove most of the char this way, and the coating that's left keeps food from sticking. For a thorough cleaning at the end of the barbecue season, spray the grill with one of the pressurized oven cleaners and follow directions for cleaning.

When you cook fatty foods on a grill, tilt the grill slightly toward you. You can prop it on a brick at the rear. The fat will run to the edge of the grid as it melts, instead of falling straight down and causing flares and smoke. Lean foods are best when basted with a little oil or butter as they cook.

Since cooking time is short on a grill, the flavor of bastes only clings to the surface of the food. For stronger flavor in grilled foods, marinate them several hours before cooking; then baste with the marinade as they cook. Very thick bastes, or bastes containing sugar burn rather easily, so use them over a low fire or use them during the last half of the cooking period.

Don't allow the coals to flame under the cooking food. Either use a drip pan or watch the fire and douse flare-ups. Flames may smudge and burn the food, leaving an unpleasant flavor and appearance.

When turning thin pieces of food such as steaks or poultry parts, many barbecue cooks prefer to use tongs rather than pierce the food, since piercing allows some of the juices to escape. If you use a fork, try to pierce an area of fat so that the seared surface of the meat itself remains intact. This no-piercing rule does not hold true for extremely fat meats or poultry. In fact, duck tastes better and less greasy if you pierce the skin often to let the fat escape.

Thick pieces of meat sometimes require such long cooking time that intense heat blackens the outside, while the inside is still raw. For these, arrange the coals in a ring at the outside edges of the food, and place a drip pan in the firebed directly underneath to catch the fat. The pan can be made of heavy aluminum foil so that it's exactly the right size.

On a covered barbecue, the cover will trap and reflect heat to cook the top and sides of roasts and poultry. If you have an open brazier, even a simple tent of foil directly over the food will trap some heat, while a complete dome of foil greatly increases efficiency. A drip pan catches fat and prevents flaring, so food requires less watching.

Meats with a large cut surface such as steaks should be started near the coals to sear the surface and seal in juices, then moved away to finish cooking. Foods that tend to disintegrate, such as ground meat patties or fish, are easier to cook if you use a hinged wire broiler for holding and turning them. Whole fish the size of salmon or alba-core should be wrapped in poultry netting or expanded metal so you don't break them when turning.

Protruding bones or fragile parts such as wing tips and the tails of whole fish may be protected from burning with a bit of foil wrapped around them or placed under them on the grill surface. In fact, if food gets too dark before it's done to your taste, slip a sheet of foil under the whole thing and continue cooking.

The grill cooking chart on pages 12 and 13 gives approximate times for cooking most grilled foods. If you use a grill thermometer, you will know the exact temperature. If you have no thermometer, you can estimate temperature with your hand. Hold it palm down near the grill and count seconds. If you're forced to remove it at three seconds, the fire is at about 350 to 400 degrees, right for steaks and chops. If it's hotter than that, wait awhile or space out the coals. If you can keep your hand in place for six to eight seconds, push the coals together, knock off the ash, or add more coals to boost the fire-power.

SMOKE COOKING

Smoke cooking and smoking are really quite distinct, although in the Chinese smoke oven, where the meat cooks in a chimney well away from the coals, the two approach each other. When foods are smoke cooked, the heat does the job, and the smoke imparts flavor. Smoking is more a curing process than a cooking process, in that the smoke causes certain chemical changes in the meat which render it edible. You can do smoke cooking in any covered barbecue in about the same time as it takes to oven cook the same things. But true smoking takes days and uses little heat.

Variety of Meat	Cut of Meat	Size or Weight	Frozen Meat Warm-up Time		Recommended Heat of Fire ①
			In Refrigerator to 40°	In Room 40° to 70°	
BEEF	Steak	1 Inch	8 Hrs.	4 Hrs.	Hot
	Steak	1½ Inches	9½ Hrs.	5 Hrs.	Hot
	Steak	2 Inches	10½ Hrs.	7 Hrs.	Medium to Hot
	Steak	2½ Inches	12 Hrs.	10 Hrs.	Medium to Hot
	Flank Steak	Whole	8 Hrs.	2½ Hrs.	Hot
	Hamburger	1 Inch	8 Hrs.	3 Hrs.	Medium to Hot
	Tenderloin	Whole	12 Hrs.	10 Hrs.	Medium
FISH	Steak	½ Inch	———		Medium
	Steak	1 Inch	———		Medium
	Fillets or Split	1 Inch	———		Medium
	Fillets or Split	1½ Inches	8 Hrs.	4 Hrs.	Medium
HAM	Slice	1 Inch	8 Hrs.	4 Hrs.	Low to Medium
	Slice	1½ Inches	9½ Hrs.	5 Hrs.	Low to Medium
LAMB	Chops or Steaks	1 Inch	8 Hrs.	4 Hrs.	Medium
	Chops or Steaks	1½ Inches	9½ Hrs.	5 Hrs.	Medium
	Chops or Steaks	2 Inches	10½ Hrs.	7 Hrs.	Medium
LOBSTER	Split	1 to 2½ Pounds	———		Medium to Hot
PORK	Chops or Steaks	1 Inch	8 Hrs.	5 Hrs.	Low to Medium
	Chops or Steaks	1½ Inches	9½ Hrs.	4 Hrs.	Low to Medium
	Chops or Steaks	2 Inches	10½ Hrs.	4 Hrs.	Low to Medium
	Spareribs	Whole	7 Hrs.	3 Hrs.	Very Low
POULTRY	Chicken	Split	10 to 12 Hrs.	6 Hrs.	Medium
	Cornish Hen	Split	8 to 11 Hrs.	2 to 3 Hrs.	Medium
	Duck	Split	11 to 12 Hrs.	6½ Hrs.	Medium to Low
	Squab	Split	8 to 11 Hrs.	2 to 3 Hrs.	Medium
	Turkey	Split (3½ to 6 lbs.)	12 to 16 Hrs.	8 Hrs.	Medium
VEAL	Steaks or Chops	1 Inch	8 Hrs.	4 Hrs.	Medium
	Steaks or Chops	1½ Inches	9½ Hrs.	5 Hrs.	Medium
VENISON	Steaks or Chops	1 Inch	8 Hrs.	4 Hrs.	Hot
	Steaks or Chops	1½ Inches	9½ Hrs.	5 Hrs.	Hot
	Steaks or Chops	2 Inches	10½ Hrs.	7 Hrs.	Medium to Hot

TEMPERATURE CHART

Approximate Time for Cooking (each side)					Comments
Very Rare	Rare	Med.-rare	Medium	Well-done	
4 Min.	5 to 6 Min.	7 Min.	7 to 8 Min.	10 Min. or More ②	① Hot fire, 375° and over; medium, 325°; slow 200° to 275°. Check with thermometer.
5 Min.	6 to 7 Min.	8 to 9 Min.	10 Min.	12 to 15 Min. ②	
7 to 8 Min.	8 to 10 Min.	10 to 15 Min.	15 to 18 Min.	20 Min. or More ②	
10 to 12 Min.	12 to 15 Min.	15 to 17 Min.	18 to 23 Min.	25 Min. or More ②	② To ascertain degree of doneness, cut steak near center with sharp knife.
3 to 4 Min.	4 to 5 Min.	5 to 6 Min.	———	——— ③	
3 Min.	4 Min.	5 Min.	6 Min.	7 Min. or More	③ Will not be tender unless very rare or rare.
10 to 12 Min.	12 to 15 Min.	15 to 17 Min.	18 to 23 Min.	——— ④	
———	———	———	———	3 to 5 Min. ⑤	④ Should be served rare.
———	———	———	———	4 to 6 Min. ⑤	
———	———	———	———	20 to 25 Min. ⑤	
———	———	———	———	25 to 30 Min. ⑤	⑤ Do not overcook lest fish become dry. When fish flakes easily with a fork it is done. Internal temperature will be about 120°.
———	———	———	———	15 to 20 Min.	
———	———	———	———	18 to 23 Min.	
———	4 to 5 Min.	6 Min.	6 to 7 Min.	8 Min. or More ⑥	
———	5 to 6 Min.	7 Min.	8 to 9 Min.	10 Min. or More ⑥	⑥ Lamb may be cooked rare to med.-rare. However, it is a matter of taste.
———	6 to 7 Min.	8 Min.	9 to 10 Min.	12 Min. or More ⑥	
———	———	———	———	15 Min. in All	
———	———	———	———	13 to 18 Min. ⑦	⑦ Pork should be well done but juicy. Cook to 180° to 185° internal temperature.
———	———	———	———	15 to 23 Min. ⑦	
———	———	———	———	20 to 30 Min. ⑦	
———	———	———	———	½ Hr. ⑧	⑧ Turn every few minutes.
———	———	———	———	35 to 45 Min. ⑨	
———	———	———	———	15 to 20 Min.	⑨ Do NOT overcook.
———	4 to 6 Min.	6 to 8 Min.	9 to 10 Min.	15 to 25 Min. ⑩	
———	———	———	———	12 to 18 Min.	⑩ For wild duck, have very hot fire and cook rare.
———	———	———	———	20 to 30 Min.	
———	———	———	———	9 to 10 Min. ⑪	
———	———	———	———	12 to 15 Min. ⑪	⑪ Veal should be well done but never dry.
4 Min.	5 to 6 Min.	6 to 7 Min.	7 to 8 Min.	10 Min. or More ⑫	
5 Min.	6 to 7 Min.	8 to 9 Min.	10 Min.	15 Min. or More ⑫	⑫ Some hunters prefer venison rare rather than well done.
7 to 8 Min.	8 to 10 Min.	10 to 15 Min.	15 to 18 Min.	20 Min. or More ⑫	

The greatest advantage of smoke cooking over spit roasting or grilling is in the definite smoky flavor. There's no doubt that smoke-cooked food was cooked over a fire of coals, for even the outside slices of a roast often take on a characteristic red coloring.

A second advantage to smoke cooking, mainly evident in cool or windy weather, is that covered cooking maintains temperature and you don't have to worry about lengthened cooking times when the breeze comes up.

Yet another advantage is that you can cook the rest of your meal in a covered barbecue at the same time you are doing a roast. Potatoes and onions will bake, and you can heat a covered casserole or roast corn. Leave the cover off already-baked beans for a smoky, crusty surface.

When you do smoke cooking, place the coals to one side or at the edges of the meat and use a drip pan. You smoke in a covered unit so that the heat and smoke are trapped as in an oven. With the coals to one side, you get plenty of heat but you won't risk burning the bottom of the food.

For the strongest smoke flavor, you must add chips or twigs of aromatic wood to your charcoal. You can even throw in small quantities of damp sawdust, but be careful not to use pine sawdust or any other soft resinous wood. You'll get an unpleasant, tarry surface on the food and a turpentine flavor. Suggestions for fire additives appear in the section on firemanship (see page 10).

Whatever you add, you have considerable choice about when to add it. For strongest flavor, put in your chips or twigs at the beginning and add more when the smoke dies down. For mild surface flavor, put in chips during the last 15 or 20 minutes.

As a rule, covered smoke cooking is sparing of charcoal. You need to maintain a temperature of 300° inside the cover, but heat doesn't escape as it does with open barbecuing, so a small amount of fuel goes a long way.

Start with about 25 to 30 briquets in a kettle or kamado, up to 50 in a box or cylinder-shaped wagon. Be prepared to add more if cooking times are very long, but the initial amount should supply adequate cooking heat for two hours or more. You should have an air temperature thermometer for accurate checking of the inside temperature.

As discussed under firemanship, you should place the coals to one side of the roast rather than underneath, and use a drip pan to prevent flaring. You use direct heat only for those foods you would normally grill, such as chicken parts or steaks. Watch these grillable items carefully since they are cooking top and bottom in a covered unit and therefore cook more quickly.

A commercially made covered barbecue, with its efficient dampers and rather deep firebed, is ideal for covered cooking; but if you'd like to try out the method on a brazier or tabletop barbecue, any cover will do. The most quickly made cover consists of a frame of 22-gauge galvanized steel wire covered with foil. Make a ring of wire the diameter of your brazier, then bend three equal half hoops of wire, attach the ends on opposite sides of the ring, and whip them together where they cross at the top. To cover the frame, run strips of foil from bottom to top, folding the vertical seams together tightly.

For small barbecues or hibachis, use a similar dome, or overturn a large kettle or Chinese wok to serve as a cover. Don't worry too much about a perfect fit since an air-tight cover will snuff out the coals.

One specialized smoker is the Chinese smoke oven. In this unit the fire is built in a fire box toward the front while the food is hung on a hook in a chimney at the back. You generally build a fire of hardwood an hour or so before you begin cooking, then stoke it with more wood from time to time during the cooking. Flames don't matter since the food is well away from the fire. Commercial units may have a thermometer on the chimney so that you can judge cooking times accurately. Dampers help control the heat. With a very slow fire, you can approach real smoking.

SPIT ROASTING

Spit cooking is the only true form of roasting. Our oven "roasts" are actually baked. The advantage to turning meat on a spit as it cooks is that the juices and bastes roll around the surface rather than dripping off into a pan or into the fire. The meat stays moist and flavorful, because it bastes itself.

Excess fat or baste will, of course, drip off the rotating food; arrange the spit so that the bottom of the roast turns toward you, while the top turns away. Arrange the fire under the back half of the roast, and place a drip pan under the front half. Fat from the turning roast falls from the portion just beginning the upswing. With a drip pan in front, you can leave the roast to cook itself without fears of flareups. Constant basting is unnecessary.

The only problem that needs careful attention in rotisserie cooking is the balance of the meat on the spit. The spit must turn evenly or there will be jerks and fast and slow rolls which will cause the meat to cook unevenly and possibly burn the heavier side, leaving the light side pale and unappetizing.

You can spit-roast very well indeed without a special balance weight, but such a weight makes the occasional problem roast easy to balance. You put the weight on the spit protruding toward the light side of the roast. If there are changes in balance during cooking due to melting fat and contracting meat, the weight can be adjusted easily to compensate. (Further tips on weights for spit roasting are given on page 9.)

The easiest roasts to balance are those of uniform shape and texture. With a rolled roast, judge the center by eye, run the spit through, tighten the holding forks, then pick up the spit, letting the ends rest in your palms loosely. If there's no tendency to roll, give the spit a quarter turn. If it's still stable, give it another quarter turn. It should rest without turning in each of these positions. You can then put it over the coals. If it does turn, respit and try again.

Small birds are fairly easy too. Truss them firmly so the wings and drumsticks stay close to the body. You can stuff the cavity with onion, garlic, celery, or a few herbs if you like. Pull down the neck skin and fix it firmly over the back with a small skewer. Then run the spit through lengthwise, catching the bird in the fork of the wishbone. Center it and tighten the holding forks. Then test the balance as above.

Irregular roasts are harder to balance, and a weight is advisable, but there are tricks to help. A turkey is so much heavier than a chicken that the holding forks need help. Truss a turkey tightly, then run the spit in at the base of the tail and diagonally through the cavity to the fork of the wishbone. Then tighten the holding forks.

Unboned rib roasts should be spitted diagonally through the meaty section. Start the spit on one cut side near the point where the ribs begin to protrude. Run it out diagonally toward the top of the other side and test the balance.

Remember that any piece of meat which is very fat will change its balance as the fat melts. If you have no adjustable weight, you will have to respit a roast that begins jerking on the turns.

As discussed in the section on spit roasting (see page 14), a spit must turn so that the top of the roast moves away from the cook and the bottom comes toward him. This makes placement of fire and drip pan easier since fat drips from the ascending side and the pan can be placed near the cook. If your spit turns in the opposite direction and you can't mount the motor on the other side to correct it, then put the coals in front (the descending side) and the pan in back (the ascending side).

If you find that protruding bones or wing tips are browning too rapidly, cover them with foil.

The chart on pages 16 and 17 gives times and temperatures for spit roasting meats, poultry, fish, and game. You should test the heat near the spit (see page 11 for directions). Heat is more variable since there is more air space between the cooking food and the fire than when you grill, so insert a meat thermometer in the center of the roast (don't let it touch bone, fat, or the spit) to be sure it is done as you like it.

Although the spit is best for large chunks of meat or for poultry, you can spit roast nearly anything if you prepare it properly. Spareribs can be folded back and forth in an undulating pattern and impaled through the folds. A large piece of liver is delicious spit roasted if you tie it into a compact piece before putting it on the spit. Whole fish can be spit roasted without danger of going to pieces if you wrap them in poultry netting or expanded metal first. However, these foods are just as good done on the grill and the effort you save in watching and basting goes into the spit preparation.

FIREPIT COOKING

Cooking underground is a method of cooking that was practiced many years ago by the Indians and by the white scouts, hunters, and trappers who roamed the country. This method of cooking beef is still favored by many barbecuers, especially at such all-out community occasions as round-ups, rodeos, fairs, and farmers' picnics. You can do pit cookery in a small way just as successfully as you can with a whole side of beef.

Essentially, cooking underground is a primitive version of roasting meat in an oven, with two important exceptions: 1) You can't peek into your "oven" to see whether the meat is done, or you may destroy the effectiveness of your coals. 2) Because the meat is tightly wrapped, it is really steam-cooked under pressure rather than roasted.

Steam-cooking keeps the meat moist while it is in the pit but is no guarantee against overcooking. It doesn't prevent overcooked meat from drying out and losing its

SPIT ROASTING TIME

Variety of Meat	Cut of Meat	Size or Weight	Frozen Meat Warm-up Time		Recommended Heat of Fire ①
			In Refrigerator to 40°	In Room 40° to 70°	
BEEF	**Standing Rib**	3 to 5 Ribs	36 to 40 Hrs.	8 Hrs.	Hot-Medium
	Rolled Rib	6 to 7 Pounds	36 to 40 Hrs.	8 Hrs.	Hot-Medium
	Spencer	8 to 10 Pounds	36 to 40 Hrs.	8 Hrs.	Hot-Medium
	Rump	3 to 5 Pounds	24 to 30 Hrs.	6 Hrs.	Medium
	Tenderloin	4 to 6 Pounds	12 to 18 Hrs.	10 Hrs.	Hot
	Sirloin	5 to 7 Pounds	18 to 24 Hrs.	8 Hrs.	Hot-Medium
FISH	**Large, Whole**	10 to 20 Pounds	30 to 40 Hrs.	12 Hrs.	Slow
HAM	**Smoked**	We do not recommend roasting cured ham over charcoal. If you wish to d‹			
LAMB	**Leg**	4 to 8 Pounds	15 to 40 Hrs.	5 to 7 Hrs.	Medium
	Rolled Shoulder	3 to 6 Pounds	15 to 30 Hrs.	4 to 6 Hrs.	Medium
	Saddle	6 to 16 Pounds	15 to 36 Hrs.	6 to 10 Hrs.	Medium
	Rack (ribs)	4 to 7 Pounds	12 to 24 Hrs.	5 to 6 Hrs.	Medium
	Baby Lamb, Kid	12 to 25 Pounds	30 to 54 Hrs.	12 to 15 Hrs.	Medium
PORK	**Loin**	5 to 14 Pounds	28 to 36 Hrs.	6 to 10 Hrs.	Medium
	Shoulder	3 to 6 Pounds	24 to 30 Hrs.	6 to 8 Hrs.	Medium
	Fresh Ham	10 to 16 Pounds	30 to 48 Hrs.	10 to 15 Hrs.	Medium
	Spareribs	1½ to 3½ Pounds	4 to 7 Hrs.	2 to 3 Hrs.	Medium to Hot
	Suckling Pig	12 to 20 Pounds	30 to 54 Hrs.	12 to 15 Hrs.	Medium
POULTRY	**Chicken**	3 to 5 Pounds	10 to 12 Hrs.	4 to 5 Hrs.	Medium
	Cornish Hen	12 oz. to 1 Pound	8 to 11 Hrs.	2 to 3 Hrs.	Medium
	Squab	10 to 14 Ounces	8 to 11 Hrs.	2 to 3 Hrs.	Medium
	Turkey	10 to 25 Pounds	15 to 36 Hrs.	8 to 10 Hrs.	Medium
	Junior Goose	4 to 7 Pounds	13 to 20 Hrs.	5 to 7 Hrs.	Medium
	Goose	8 to 15 Pounds	20 to 30 Hrs.	6 to 9 Hrs.	Medium
	Duckling	4 to 6 Pounds	13 to 18 Hrs.	5 to 7 Hrs.	Medium
VEAL	**Leg**	8 to 14 Pounds	24 to 36 Hrs.	7 to 10 Hrs.	Medium
	Loin	10 to 13 Pounds	20 to 30 Hrs.	6 to 9 Hrs.	Medium
	Shoulder (rolled)	3 to 5 Pounds	15 to 24 Hrs.	4 to 6 Hrs.	Medium
VENISON	**Leg**	9 to 12 Pounds	20 to 40 Hrs.	7 to 10 Hrs.	Hot-Medium
	Saddle	5 to 7 Pounds	15 to 24 Hrs.	4 to 6 Hrs.	Hot-Medium
	Shoulder	12 to 18 Pounds	18 to 40 Hrs.	8 to 12 Hrs.	Medium

AND TEMPERATURE CHART

Approximate Time for Cooking					Comments
Very Rare 120°-130°	Rare 130°-135°	Med.-rare 135°-145°	Medium 145°-155°	Well-done 155°180°	
½ to 2¼ Hrs.	1¾ to 2¼ Hrs.	2 to 2¾ Hrs.	2½ to 3 Hrs.	3 to 4½ Hrs.②	① Hot fire, 325° or over; medium, 250 to 300°; slow, 150 to 225°. Check with thermometer.
¼ to 2½ Hrs.	2 to 2¾ Hrs.	2¼ to 3 Hrs.	2¾ to 3¼ Hrs.	3¼ to 5 Hrs.②	
½ to 2½ Hrs.	2½ to 3 Hrs.	2¾ to 3½ Hrs.	3 to 4 Hrs.	3½ to 5½ Hrs.②	
¼ to 1¾ Hrs.	1½ to 2 Hrs.	1¾ to 2½ Hrs.	2½ to 3 Hrs.	3 to 4½ Hrs.	
5 to 40 Min.	35 to 45 Min.	45 to 60 Min.	1 to 1¼ Hrs.	1 to 2 Hrs.③	② Start with very hot fire; let it burn down to medium.
to 1½ Hrs.	1¼ to 1¾ Hrs.	1¾ to 2¼ Hrs.	2¼ to 3 Hrs.	3 to 4 Hrs.④	
Cook to about 120° internal temperature.⑤					
so, follow timing for fresh ham (below).					③ If meat is larded (wrapped in fat), it will take somewhat longer to cook.
0 to 65 Min.	1 to 1¼ Hrs.	1¼ to 1½ Hrs.	1½ to 2 Hrs.	2 Hrs. or More ⑥	
0 to 65 Min.	1 to 1¼ Hrs.	1¼ to 1½ Hrs.	1½ to 2 Hrs.	2 Hrs. or More ⑥	
———	¾ to 1¼ Hrs.	1 to 1½ Hrs.	1¼ to 1¾ Hrs.	2 Hrs. or More ⑥	④ Handle fire as for rib roast, above.
———	¾ to 1 Hr.	1 to 1¼ Hrs.	1¼ to 1½ Hrs.	2 Hrs. or More ⑥	
———	———	———	2 to 2½ Hrs.	2½ to 3½ Hrs.	
———	———	———	———	2 to 4 Hrs.⑦	⑤ Thawing time varies, depending upon shape of fish.
———	———	———	———	2 to 3½ Hrs.⑦	
———	———	———	———	4 to 6 Hrs.⑦	
———	———	———	———	1 to 1½ Hrs.⑦	
———	———	———	———	3 to 4 Hrs.⑦	⑥ Some believe lamb is tenderer and more flavorsome when cooked rare.
———	———	———	———	1 to 1½ Hrs.⑧	
———	———	———	———	¾ to 1 Hr.⑧	
———	———	———	———	¾ to 1 Hr.⑧	
———	———	———	———	2 to 4 Hrs.⑧	⑦ Pork should be cooked to 180° to 185° internal temperture.
———	———	———	———	1¾ to 2½ Hrs.	
———	———	———	———	2 to 3 Hrs.	
———	———	———	———	1 to 2 Hrs.⑨	⑧ Eviscerated weight. Use leg joint test to determine doneness.
———	———	———	———	2 to 3 Hrs.	
———	———	———	———	1½ to 2½ Hrs.	
———	———	———	———	¾ to 1½ Hrs.	⑨ Whole wild duck cooks in 20 to 30 minutes to very rare stage.
to 1¼ Hrs.	1¼ to 1½ Hrs.	1½ to 1¾ Hrs.	1¾ to 2¼ Hrs.	2 Hrs. or More	
0 to 65 Min.	1 to 1¼ Hrs.	1¼ to 1½ Hrs.	1½ to 2 Hrs.	2 Hrs. or More	
———	1¼ to 1½ Hrs.	1½ to 1¾ Hrs.	1¾ to 2¼ Hrs.	2 Hrs. or More	

flavor as soon as it is exposed to the air. In pit barbecuing, meat doesn't get the kind of searing that seals in juices when you roast it in the oven or cook it over an open fire.

How do you control the process? You can't read dials on the oven or on a meat thermometer. You have to control the cooking by the way you handle the fire and by your timing. The important elements are these: size of the pit; kind of wood; length of time the fire burns before you put on the meat; size, weight, kind, and preparation of the meat used for cooking underground; covering of the meat and the fire; cooking time.

The Pit and the Fire

The experts on pit barbecuing don't agree among themselves as to the proper size of the pit. Actually, you can figure out the best size for your own operation if you understand the method.

As for the length and width obviously these dimensions should be large enough so you can spread the meat out on the coals, in one large package or several small ones. In addition, there should be a little extra space all around the meat, so that heat from the outer coals will cook the outside edges of the meat. On a small-scale job, you might cheat a little on the outside edge and make the pit about 1½ feet wide. For easy handling of the meat and general convenience, a 3-foot width is about maximum. Length can be anything required by the quantity of the meat.

To determine the depth, just add up the thickness of each layer you intend to put in the pit.

Many experts like to line the bottom (and sometimes part way up the sides) with bricks or with large round

stones, which should be hard and dry, without crevices or porous sections holding water that might later make the rock explode under steam pressure.

When the pit is ready for cooking, the first thing you must add is the bed of coals; recommended depths range from 1 to 2 feet (depends on cooking time you favor). Next comes the meat; some put it right on the coals, and others bank the fire and protect the meat from possible burning with about an inch of pre-heated dry sand. Finally comes the layer of dirt (right on the meat package or on a cover of metal or canvas); recommended depth is 1 foot.

Add up these figures and you get a depth of about 2½ to 5 feet. It varies according to the depth of the bed of coals, the size of the meat packages, and, if you use a cover, whether you put it right on the meat or a few inches above it. (If you use galvanized iron, burn off the coating beforehand so it won't add an undesirable flavor to the meat.)

If you cook a pot of beans underground, you can use a smaller, shallower pit. The bed of coals may be as little as 6 inches deep, although a little extra depth won't matter.

What Kind of Wood

With the pit dug, the next step is to prepare the fire. The aim is to prepare a bed of coals of the approximate size and consistency of charcoal. All the pieces of wood should be burning or be thoroughly charred. Any uncharred pieces should be removed before the meat is placed on top.

Wood has to be fairly hard if it is to burn slowly enough to pile up a bed of coals. Anything as soft and fast-burning as pine is likely to leave ashes and very little else.

Favorite woods for this purpose include oak, alder, hickory, mesquite, ironwood, and the wood from most orchard trees—walnut, pecan, apple, orange, lemon. Needless to say, the wood should be thoroughly dry. It burns best if pieces aren't more than about 4 inches thick.

Timing the Fire

When you stoke your preliminary fire, you are really heating up an oven—the bottom and sides of your pit—so that the stored heat will continue to cook for the next several hours. The principle is very much like that of the igloo-shaped Mexican oven, in which you build your fire, then scrape it all out and do your cooking with the heat stored in the walls.

In the pit barbecue, you should keep replenishing the fire until the bed of coals reaches the desired depth. Each expert has his own timing on this step, but the majority would agree that 3 to 6 hours should be enough to develop a 1 to 2-foot depth of coals. Less than 3 hours may not pre-heat your "oven" enough; more than 6 hours may get it too hot.

Preparing the Meat

Standard practice is to wrap the chunks of meat in one or more layers of closely woven white cloth, parchment, or foil, and tie with twine; then wrap in one or more thicknesses of burlap and secure with wire. Each package is sprinkled or doused quickly in water before it goes on the coals.

Before wrapping, you can use any of the seasonings you might use with a roast. You can sprinkle the meat with liquid and dry seasonings or you can inject marinades with a syringe.

The traditional large-scale barbecue calls for whole quarters or whole sides of beef. But without a whole corps of meat cutters on duty, it is difficult to carve such huge pieces fast enough to serve the meat while it is still hot. For this reason many now prefer to bone the meat beforehand and tie it in reasonably small rolls that can be carved fast and easily. You can keep each piece wrapped until the cutter is ready to go to work on it. This method is definitely best for any family-size pit barbecue.

Covering the Pit

The most primitive method is to pile the layer of dirt right on the meat packages—and do it fast before they have a chance to burn. A good idea here is to wrap a length of thick but soft wire around each package and let it stick up above the layer of dirt; you'll have no trouble pulling out each piece of meat and won't have to grapple for it with either a shovel or pitchfork.

For a more sanitary job, and especially if you'd like to use your burlap again for the same purpose, put a cover over the meat before throwing on the dirt. Canvas is used occasionally, but by far the most popular covering is thick sheet iron or corrugated galvanized iron (with the coating well burned off).

Some improvise a frame inside the pit in order to get the cover close to the meat. Others put pipes or rods across the top of the pit to support the cover; then they mound up the dirt on top.

In either case, work fast. Shovel dirt until you see no smoke or steam escaping. Some prefer to stamp on the dirt as it is being piled up. Others use a little water and seal the top with mud.

About every half hour, make an inspection to see that no steam is escaping. If it is, cover with dirt and stamp it down.

Cooking Time

Here is the supreme test of artistry. You have to know your fire and what it will do. You also have to gauge time by the size of your pieces of meat, much as you gauge oven cooking times by the size of your roast. Generally, meat in 6 to 10-pound pieces will require about 5 hours cooking time; in 20-pound pieces, 8 to 10 hours; hindquarters of beef (100 to 150 pounds, dressed), 15 to 18 hours; pots of beans, 4 to 6 hours.

The theory is that if your preliminary firing is right, the heat will subside after the first few hours of cooking is done. You do have some latitude, but don't trust this theory too far.

On your first trial, you'll have to do some experimenting and adjusting to fit these directions to your cooking job.

It's worth noting that most reliable experts in this field are not improvisers at all. After trial and error, they've learned exactly what to do (pit, fire, and timing) with a certain quantity of meat. They have developed a set routine and they know it well, and they don't mind repeating it over and over again.

COOKING ON SKEWERS

Skewer cookery is probably the most versatile barbecue method, and can adapt to any size barbecue. A tiny hibachi with just a few coals will grill whole prawns or small chunks of meat, fish, or poultry. On hotter fires, cut the pieces bigger, up to 1½ to 2 inches on a side, and push them more tightly together. Packed skewers cook more slowly and center chunks are pinker and juicier.

If you want vegetables or fruits on the skewer with the meat, use firm ones that cook slowly, or use some of the skewers for meat only, others for the quicker-cooking vegetables.

For appetizers, buy slivers of bamboo in an Oriental store and soak them in water for awhile before use to keep them from burning.

Certain foods, such as pork chunks, should be pre-cooked in the oven before skewering so that they will be cooked when their skewer companions are ready.

When you skewer chunks of fish, leave the skin on. It will help hold the flesh together when the fish is completely cooked.

You can baste skewered foods with butter, oil, or a marinade, or you can create self-basting skewers by threading a bacon slice over and under each food chunk in an undulating pattern.

As you prepare various foods for skewer cooking ahead of time, keep in mind their cooking requirements. Those that just need heating—fruits, canned or pre-cooked foods—can be skewered in larger portions than those that require cooking. Group longer cooking foods, such as meats, together; add foods to be cooked quickly or just heated at the end of cooking time.

Skewer cooking more than any other form of barbecuing lends itself to do-it-yourself parties. Have an assortment of food already cut and arranged on plates. Let guests fill their own skewers with a mixture that pleases them. If you're using one large barbecue, it's best to do the actual cooking yourself, but you can also fire up several smaller ones so that the traffic is divided.

Arni Souvlakia
SKEWER-COOKED

Here's a skewer entrée idea from Greece. You might alternate the lamb cubes with small tomatoes and green pepper slices. Serve it with rice Pilaf.

    3 pounds boneless leg or shoulder of lamb,
        cut into 1½-inch cubes
        Lemon juice
    1 tablespoon salt
    1 teaspoon pepper
    1 teaspoon oregano
        Olive oil

Dip each lamb cube in lemon juice. Combine salt with pepper and oregano; sprinkle over the meat cubes. Thread meat on skewers. Broil over charcoal until the meat is brown but still juicy, brushing with olive oil two or three times. Makes 6 servings.

Chinese Pork Appetizers
SKEWER-COOKED

Three sweet spices—cinnamon, cloves, and anise—flavor the pork for these unusual hot appetizers. The meat is barbecued with pieces of pineapple and green pepper.

¼ cup soy sauce
2 tablespoons salad oil
2 cloves garlic, mashed
1 small dried, hot chile pepper, crushed
½ teaspoon sugar
¼ teaspoon anise seed
⅛ teaspoon cinnamon
⅛ teaspoon cloves
1 pound lean pork, cut into bite-sized
 strips or cubes
1 small fresh pineapple
1 medium-sized green pepper

Combine the soy sauce, salad oil, garlic, chile pepper, sugar, anise, cinnamon, and cloves in a bowl. Add the pork and stir gently to coat each piece with the marinade. Refrigerate meat 1 to 2 hours, stirring occasionally. String pork on skewers with bite-sized pieces of fresh pineapple and green pepper. Grill about 5 inches from the heat for 7 to 10 minutes, turning once. Serve hot.

Lamb in Onion Juice
SKEWER-COOKED

You can alternate pieces of bacon, onion, green peppers, or even very small tomatoes with these lamb cubes.

2 pounds lean lamb, cut in 1-inch cubes
2 medium-sized onions
½ cup salad oil
1 bay leaf
1 teaspoon salt
½ teaspoon thyme
 Pinch of sage
3 whole black peppers, crushed
1 cup Sherry or dry red wine

Put lamb cubes into an earthen bowl. Run the two onions through the food grinder, using the finest blade. Squeeze the onion pulp through a small muslin sack or cloth onto the meat. Add the oil, bay leaf, salt, thyme, sage, and whole black peppers, working them into the meat. Add the wine and marinate overnight. Then string the meat on skewers and grill to your taste.

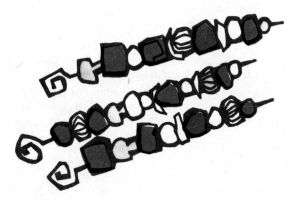

Beef Skirts-Kebab
SKEWER-COOKED

Whole skirt steaks resemble flank steaks, but are smaller. Two will adequately serve four persons.

2 whole skirt steaks
¼ cup salad or olive oil
1 cup dry red wine
1 clove garlic, crushed
1 medium-sized onion, minced or grated
½ teaspoon pepper
2 tablespoons soy sauce
2 tablespoons prepared mustard
 Fresh mushroom caps, quartered; onions,
 green peppers, and tomatoes as desired

Cut each skirt steak in half lengthwise. Combine salad oil, wine, garlic, onion, pepper, soy sauce, and mustard. Marinate the steaks in this mixture for at least 5 hours—the longer the better.

When the charcoal fire is ready, thread the meat on metal skewers in a ribbon style, alternating with mushrooms and other vegetables used.

The fire should be 6 to 8 inches from skewers. Barbecue steaks about 5 minutes on each side. To serve, remove the skewers. Makes 4 servings.

Beef-Oyster Appetizers
SKEWER-COOKED

Oyster sauce (bottled like soy sauce) is a necessary ingredient for this hot appetizer. The sauce may be purchased in most Oriental markets.

¼ cup oyster sauce
2 tablespoons salad oil
2 tablespoons soy sauce
1 clove garlic, mashed
2 green onions, chopped
¼ teaspoon sugar
1 pound beef sirloin, cut into bite-sized
 strips or cubes
½ pound fresh mushrooms,
 washed and drained
1 can (6½ oz.) whole water
 chestnuts, drained
3 green onions, cut into 1-inch pieces

Combine the oyster sauce, salad oil, soy sauce, garlic, chopped onion, and sugar in a bowl. Marinate the beef and mushrooms in this mixture for 1 to 2 hours in the refrigerator. Then string meat, mushrooms, water chestnuts, and pieces of green onion on skewers. Barbecue about 5 inches from the heat for 5 minutes, turning once. Serve hot.

Sweetbreads and Steak Brochette
SKEWER-COOKED

This French skewer combination of top round steak and poached sweetbreads is enlivened with tarragon-lemon butter in two ways: first, brushed over the meat while it grills, and second, spooned over the kebabs at the table.

1 pound sweetbreads
1 quart water
1 tablespoon lemon juice
1 teaspoon salt
1 pound top round steak,
    cut ¾ inch thick in 1-inch squares
2 strips bacon
6 fresh mushrooms
    (1½ inches in diameter, preferably)
½ cup (¼ lb.) butter or margarine
½ teaspoon grated lemon peel
2 teaspoons lemon juice
¼ teaspoon salt
1 tablespoon finely chopped parsley
¼ teaspoon dried tarragon, crumbled

Wash the sweetbreads in cold water, then soak for 2 to 3 hours, changing the water several times. Drain, cover with about 1 quart cold water (enough to cover them) and add the 1 tablespoon lemon juice and 1 teaspoon salt. Bring to a boil and simmer for 15 minutes. Drain and plunge into cold water for 5 minutes to cool; drain again.

With a sharp knife and your fingers, remove as much white connecting membrane as possible. Then cut sweetbreads into pieces similar in size to the steak squares.

Cut bacon crosswise into ¾-inch pieces and precook partially under the broiler, just until limp. Using 6 skewers, alternate steak squares, bacon, and sweetbreads on a skewer and end with a mushroom cap (cut off stems and use in another recipe).

For tarragon butter, cream butter until light and fluffy. Blend in lemon peel, the 2 teaspoons lemon juice, ¼ teaspoon salt, the parsley, and tarragon. Spoon into a sauce bowl.

Place skewers over medium barbecue coals and grill for about 10 to 12 minutes for rare meat, turning to brown all sides. While grilling, brush meat several times with the seasoned butter. Serve with the herb butter to spoon over as desired. Makes 6 servings.

Kebab Sauce

You can make this sauce in quantity and store it in the refrigerator for use on kebabs of beef, pork, poultry, and fish with pronounced flavors.

1 can (10½ oz.) condensed tomato soup
    Water
    Oil or shortening
1 teaspoon dry mustard
1 teaspoon sugar (firmly packed brown,
    or granulated)
1 teaspoon salt
2 teaspoons chile powder
3 to 4 tablespoons wine or vinegar
1 onion, finely chopped
1 large clove garlic, finely chopped
    Pinch rosemary
1 tablespoon liquid smoke
    Worcestershire
    Paprika
    Pepper

Pour soup into a pan; fill can about three-fourths full of water, and add enough shortening or oil to bring water to top of the can; pour into saucepan. Add mustard, sugar, salt, chile powder, wine or vinegar, chopped onion, chopped garlic, rosemary, liquid smoke, and Worcestershire, paprika, and pepper to taste.

Heat to boiling and cook for about 5 minutes, or until all ingredients are well blended. Makes about 2¾ cups of sauce.

Shish Koftesi
SKEWER-COOKED

Ground meat is used for these Turkish kebabs. It is formed into sausage shapes for threading on the skewers.

2 pounds ground lean lamb or beef
1 cup finely minced onion
3 eggs
1 teaspoon whole thyme
2 teaspoons salt
1 clove garlic, puréed
    Olive oil

Combine ground lamb or beef, onion, eggs, thyme, salt, and garlic; mix well. Chill. Form into sausage-shaped pieces about 3 inches long and 1 inch in diameter; thread lengthwise on skewers, two or three on each skewer. Brush with olive oil and grill over hot coals for 8 to 10 minutes, turning to brown all sides. Makes 6 to 8 servings.

East Indian Saté
SKEWER-COOKED

This thick marinade has a mild peanut flavor that is delicious with veal, pork, or chicken; serve the remaining marinade as a sauce over the cooked meat. Consider alternating the meat with chunks of pineapple that have been dipped in melted butter.

    1 tablespoon ground coriander
    1 tablespoon salt
    ½ teaspoon freshly ground pepper
    1 cup chopped onion
    2 cloves garlic, peeled
    ½ cup soy sauce
    ¼ cup lime or lemon juice
    ½ cup peanut butter
    ¼ cup brown sugar
    ½ cup peanut or salad oil
      Dash cayenne or liquid hot-pepper
      seasoning
    2 pounds meat (boneless veal leg or shoulder,
      or boned chicken) cut into 1-inch cubes

Combine coriander, salt, pepper, onion, garlic, soy sauce, lime or lemon juice, peanut butter, brown sugar, peanut or salad oil, and cayenne or liquid hot-pepper seasoning. Whirl smooth in a blender. Marinate the meat in this mixture for 1 to 2 hours. String on skewers. Grill over hot coals until brown but not dry, about 3 to 4 minutes on each side. Serve with the remaining marinade. Makes 6 to 8 servings.

Indonesian Satés
SKEWER-COOKED

Satés, or skewered grilled meats, are sold from little carts at public gatherings in Indonesia as hot dogs are sold at American ball games. This recipe for Indonesian satés uses pork, but chicken, beef, or veal is equally suitable.

    1 large onion, ground
    4 cloves garlic, minced or crushed
    2 teaspoons pepper
    ¾ cup lime juice
    1 cup soy sauce
    ½ cup dark molasses
    1 cup salad oil
    5 pounds boneless lean pork,
      cut in 1 to 1½-inch cubes

Make sauce by combining onion, garlic, pepper, lime juice, soy sauce, molasses, and salad oil. Force this mixture through a sieve or whirl in a blender. Marinate meat in this sauce for 3 to 4 hours. Skewer meat on bamboo sticks, 3 or 4 pieces to each stick. Grill over charcoal until meat is brown and crisp on all sides — 15 to 20 minutes. Do not overcook, or the meat will be dry. Heat

remaining marinade and serve with the saté. Makes 25 servings.

Lamb Rolls
with Curry Honey Glaze
SKEWER-COOKED

Lamb shoulder rolls are tender and juicy; delicious when barbecued. If you don't see the rolls at your market, ask your meatman to make them from boneless lamb shoulder chops; they are cut 1 to 1½ inches thick and held with wooden skewers.

    6 lamb shoulder rolls,
      each about ¾ pound
      Quartered green pepper pieces,
      parboiled 1 minute in boiling water
      Melted butter or salad oil

Remove wooden skewers from lamb rolls; alternate the rolls on long metal skewers with the parboiled green pepper pieces. Brush the pepper with melted butter or salad oil. Grill over hot coals for 5 to 10 minutes on each side or until meat is done to your liking. During the last 2 minutes of cooking, brush on both sides with curry honey glaze (recipe follows). Serve hot. Makes 6 servings.

Curry Honey Glaze

    ¼ cup honey
    2 tablespoons salad oil
    2 tablespoons lemon juice
    ¼ teaspoon curry powder
    ½ teaspoon salt
      Dash coarse-ground pepper

Combine the honey, salad oil, lemon juice, curry powder, salt, and pepper.

Pakistani Kebabs
SKEWER-COOKED

The spice mixture in the marinade for these kebabs is similar to a Pakistani curry. Use beef, lamb, or chicken — or some of each. If you plan to serve a combination of meats, put each kind on an individual skewer.

1½ cups yogurt
  1 small onion, chopped
  1 clove garlic, crushed
  1 teaspoon chopped fresh ginger
    (or ¼ teaspoon ground ginger)
  1 small dried hot chile pepper, crushed
  ½ teaspoon cumin seed, crushed
  ½ teaspoon ground nutmeg
  ¼ teaspoon ground cardamom
  ¼ teaspoon salt
  ⅛ teaspoon ground cinnamon
  ⅛ teaspoon ground cloves
  ⅛ teaspoon coarsely ground black pepper
  2 pounds boneless lean beef sirloin or lamb
    (shoulder or leg), cut in 1¼-inch cubes,
    or 5 whole chicken breasts, skinned, boned,
    and cut in bite-sized pieces

To make the marinade, combine the yogurt, onion, garlic, ginger, chile pepper, cumin, nutmeg, cardamom, salt, cinnamon, cloves, and black pepper. Stir meat into marinade (keep meats separate if you use several so you can skewer and cook them separately). Cover and refrigerate overnight.

Remove meat from marinade and string on skewers. Barbecue until browned and just tender — about 15 minutes for lamb and beef, 10 minutes for chicken. Makes about 6 servings.

Skewered Veal Barbecue
SKEWER-COOKED

When making these kebabs, if you have any pineapple left over drain it well; sauté the pieces in a small amount of butter until lightly browned and serve as an accompaniment.

⅓ cup soy sauce
  1 large onion, chopped
  2 tablespoons salad or olive oil
  1 tablespoon dried oregano
  2 or 3 veal steaks, ½ to ¾ inch thick
    Dry red wine
  1 can (1 lb., 13 oz.) sliced pineapple

Mix together the soy sauce, onion, oil, and oregano. Cut the veal steaks into 1 to 1½-inch squares, depending on the thickness of your skewers. Put the veal squares in a bowl, pour in the marinade, then add enough wine to cover the meat. Let the meat marinate all day and turn it in the marinade from time to time. Cut the pineapple slices into quarters.

About 2 hours before time to barbecue, string the meat on the skewers with a piece of pineapple between every two pieces of meat. You'll have to work carefully as the pineapple might split if skewers are too large. Arrange the skewers on a shallow pan, pour over the sauce and marinate, turning occasionally, until time to barbecue over coals. Barbecuing takes about 20 minutes in all, turning 4 times. Baste with the marinade when you turn skewers. This fills 6 good-sized skewers.

Skewer Combinations

If you are wondering what foods complement each other on skewers, here are some tried and true combinations:
• Pork cubes, pineapple chunks, green pepper squares, sweet potato squares.
• Steak cubes, brown-and-serve bread chunks, mushroom caps, tomatoes.
• Prunes, brown-and-serve sausage, small onions, spiced crab apples.
• Ham cubes, thick-sliced banana, sweet potatoes.
• Figs stuffed with anchovies; ripe olives, salami cubes, brown-and-serve rolls.
• Polish sausage, cherry tomatoes, eggplant cubes, stuffed green olives.
• Cheese cubes and luncheon meat, cut in quarters, and threaded alternately with mushrooms or ripe olives.
• Meatballs, onions, cherry tomatoes, mushrooms.
• Knackwurst, small onions, potato or zucchini slices.
• Turkey cubes, pineapple chunks, ripe olives, sweet potatoes.
• Ham cubes, corn on the cob, cheese wrapped in refrigerated biscuits, stuffed olives.

· Shrimps, pineapple cubes, green pepper squares, cherry tomatoes.

· Fresh albacore cubes, stuffed olives, zucchini slices, small onions, potatoes wrapped in bacon.

· Liver cubes, cherry tomatoes, eggplant cubes, bacon squares, onion slices.

Chicken Liver Kebabs
SKEWER-COOKED

If you like chicken livers, here's an easy and delicious way to skewer-cook them.

18 chicken livers
   Salt and pepper
6 slices bacon
   Mushrooms
   Olive oil
   Fresh bread crumbs
   Butter, melted
   Lemon juice
   Parsley

Wash chicken livers, and dry well with clean cloth. Sprinkle with salt and pepper. Cut each liver in half. Broil bacon slices, one minute to each side, and cut each slice into 6 pieces.

Take skewers, run one through center of liver slice, a piece of bacon, and a mushroom until all skewers are filled. Roll in olive oil, dip in fresh bread crumbs, and grill over hot coals.

Arrange skewers on a hot dish, and over them pour melted butter to which lemon juice and chopped parsley have been added. Makes 6 servings.

If you use round steak, you may want to prepare it with instant meat tenderizer, following the directions given on the package. Wrap a lobster tail around a piece of beef and thread the skewer through the thick end of the lobster tail, the beef cube, then the end of the lobster tail. You can put three of these combinations onto each of two long skewers. To make the basting sauce, combine the wine, salad oil, and lemon juice. Grill the kebabs over hot coals for 8 to 12 minutes, or until lobster flakes when tested with a fork and beef is done to your liking. Baste while cooking. Serve hot with lemon wedges and Tomato Béarnaise (recipe follows). Makes 6 servings.

Giant Beef-Lobster Kebabs
SKEWER-COOKED

Meat for six cooks on two skewers when you use this giant shish kebab combination. If you like, you can skewer parboiled vegetables and continue cooking them over the hot coals (see page 88). There's also a special Béarnaise sauce.

1½ to 2 pounds top sirloin or top round steak,
   cut in 2-inch cubes
   Unseasoned meat tenderizer (optional)
3 frozen lobster tails (about 1½ lbs.),
   split lengthwise and thawed
⅓ cup dry white wine
⅓ cup salad oil
1 tablespoon lemon juice
   Lemon wedges
   Tomato Béarnaise (recipe follows)

Tomato Béarnaise

3 egg yolks
1½ tablespoons tarragon vinegar
¾ cup butter
½ teaspoon salt
½ teaspoon tarragon
3 tablespoons finely chopped parsley
2 tablespoons tomato purée

Combine the egg yolks and tarragon vinegar in an electric blender container. Melt butter; turn blender on high speed and immediately pour in the hot butter in a steady stream. Add salt, tarragon, and finely chopped parsley; whirl until blended, about 30 seconds. Mix in tomato purée. Makes about 2 cups sauce.

BEEF

There's drama in a steak sizzling over a barbecue fire or a succulent roast turning on a rotisserie. While you don't need to be an expert to barbecue beef, it is important to understand some of the basic facts. Thick steaks, chops, or flat roasts are best for grill cooking; choose more compact roasts for the rotisserie.

Roasts are best cooked covered, either in a barbecue with a hood or on a grill with a blanket of heavy foil over the meat (see page 14 for directions).

While some cuts of beef are extremely tender and flavorful, others are best tenderized or marinated for additional flavor.

You'll notice that the internal temperatures suggested for beef in this book are lower than those formerly considered standard. This is due to the ever-improving quality of beef in our markets, as well as the increasing popularity of less well done meat. Use a good meat thermometer to test the doneness of a roast or even a thick steak. When properly placed in the center of the thickest muscle, 130° indicates the meat is rare—pink throughout, yet firm; at 140°, the meat is brown part way through, yet pink in the middle and still juicy; by 150°, most roasts will be evenly browned throughout, well done, yet still fairly juicy.

Retained heat will cause the temperature of a large roast to rise; remove meat from the barbecue when it's several degrees below the temperature you prefer.

Hawaiian Beef Appetizers
SKEWER-COOKED

These Hawaiian beef cubes are simple to make and can be cooked over a tiny hibachi.

2-inch piece fresh, peeled ginger, sliced
2 cloves garlic, mashed
2 small onions, chopped
1 cup soy sauce
4 tablespoons sugar
8 small dried, hot chile peppers
2 tablespoons red wine vinegar
4 teaspoons cornstarch
½ cup water
2 pounds beef sirloin,
    cut into bite-sized pieces

In small pan, combine ginger, garlic, onions, soy sauce, sugar, chile peppers, and wine vinegar. Cook over medium heat until slightly thick, about 20 minutes. Blend cornstarch and water. Gradually stir into sauce and cook, stirring until clear and thickened. Pour mixture through a wire strainer, pressing out all the juices, and discard the pulp; cool. Add beef pieces to marinade and allow to stand, covered, for 2 hours. Thread 2 or 3 pieces of meat on each skewer; barbecue over hot coals. Makes about 4 dozen appetizers.

Shallot Sauce

The French consider the shallot (a small onion-like bulb) to be a choice flavoring ingredient in many dishes. It's the important flavor in this quickly-made sauce to serve with barbecued beef steak.

For each steak, melt 1½ teaspoons butter in a frying pan. Add 1½ tablespoons chopped shallots and sauté until shallots are soft, but not browned. Add 2 tablespoons dry red wine and reduce the liquid over high heat until most of the liquid is gone. Serve at once over piping hot meat. Makes enough sauce for 1 steak.

Soy-Lemon Marinade for Beef

A six-pound roast can be marinated up to three days in this marinade, using a heavy plastic bag for the marinating process.

½ cup soy sauce
½ cup lemon juice
½ cup salad oil
1 bay leaf
½ teaspoon seasoned pepper
1 clove garlic, crushed

Combine soy sauce, lemon juice, salad oil, bay leaf, pepper, and garlic. Put meat and marinade in a heavy plastic bag. Tie bag securely; place in a bowl. Refrigerate overnight or up to 3 days, turning frequently. Drain meat before roasting. Baste meat with marinade, if you wish. Makes enough marinade for a 6-pound roast.

Mexican Sauces for Beef

These three Mexican sauces are found in many delicious Mexican dishes. Each is also very good served with barbecued beef.

Red Chile Sauce

Place 6 ounces (about 10 to 12) whole dried chiles pasillas or California chiles (or 3 ounces of each) on a baking sheet. Bake in a hot oven (400°) for 3 or 4 minutes. Remove from oven, let cool to touch, then remove and discard stems, seeds, and any pink pithy material inside the chiles. Rinse in cool water, drain briefly, then cover chiles with 3 cups hot water; let stand 1 hour.

Place chiles in an electric blender and add just enough of the water to blend; whirl until smooth (or rub chiles through a wire strainer, or mash to a paste in a mortar and pestle). Add remaining water, ¼ cup tomato sauce or tomato paste, 1 small clove garlic, ¼ cup salad oil, 1½ teaspoons salt, 1 teaspoon oregano, and ¼ teaspoon ground cumin. Simmer sauce gently for 10 minutes, stirring occasionally. You can freeze this sauce. Makes 3½ cups. (Thin sauce to any desired consistency with meat or poultry broth.)

Fresh Tomato and Green Chile Sauce

Peel and finely chop 6 medium-sized tomatoes. Mix with ½ cup (or more) thinly sliced or diced canned green chiles, ⅓ cup minced onion, 1 teaspoon salt, and as many minced chile jalapeños (or other hot chiles) as please your taste (about 1 jalapeño to each cup of sauce will make it noticeably hot). Makes 3 cups.

Guacamole

Mash 2 large peeled and pitted ripe avocados with a fork until fairly smooth. Blend in 1 small mashed or minced garlic clove, 2 or 3 tablespoons lemon or lime juice (or to taste), ¼ teaspoon ground coriander (optional), dash of cayenne, and salt to taste. For a touch of heat, add 2 or 3 chopped canned green chiles. Makes about 1⅔ cups.

Ginger Beef Teriyaki
SKEWER-COOKED

Ginger lovers will savor this version of the popular teriyaki treatment for barbecuing steak.

2 pounds sirloin steak, sliced ¼ inch thick
½ cup soy sauce
1 tablespoon grated fresh ginger or
  1 tablespoon ginger juice
¼ cup sake or Sherry
1 clove garlic, puréed
1 teaspoon to 3 tablespoons sugar

Marinate steak for about 1 hour in a mixture of soy sauce, fresh ginger or ginger juice (available now in some markets), sake or Sherry, garlic, and sugar (according to taste). Drain; weave meat on skewers, using one skewer for each strip of meat. Cook quickly, 1 to 2 minutes on each side, over hot coals, basting with the marinade. Do not overcook. Makes about 6 servings.

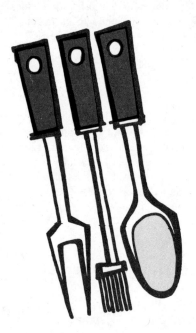

Tenderloin Steak Casanova
GRILL-COOKED

The next time you feel like splurging, try this dish on your non-dieting friends. Serve the sauced steaks with crusty rolls and a simple salad.

Sprinkle 6 tenderloin steaks (cut 1 inch thick) with salt and pepper; then brush with olive oil. Let stand while you ready a charcoal fire and the sauce. For the sauce, heat 4 ounces pâté de foie gras with ¼ cup cream Sherry or Marsala in a large frying pan, stirring until smooth. Grill the steaks to your liking; then put them in the frying pan on top of the sauce. Add ¼ cup warm cognac; then flame. As the burning cognac blends with the sauce, spoon it over the steaks and serve at once. Makes 6 servings.

Filet Mignon Aubergine
GRILL-COOKED

If you like your beef rare, put the eggplant slices on the grill before starting to cook the beef.

For each serving allow a 1-inch-thick steak cut from the small end of a beef fillet, and one crosswise slice of eggplant cut about ¾ inch thick. With olive oil or melted butter, generously brush the cut sides of the eggplant slices and lightly brush the beef fillets; sprinkle with salt.
    Prepare this sauce while coals heat: For 4 servings, whip ½ cup heavy cream until stiff and blend in 1 table-spoon prepared Dijon mustard, 3 tablespoons tomato catsup or purée, and salt to taste. Chill until ready to use.
    Place eggplant on grill about 5 inches above medium-hot coals. Cook for 10 to 12 minutes, turning occasionally with a spatula and basting with more oil or melted butter. Cook the beef on the same grill, allowing 4 minutes to a side for rare meat, 7 minutes to a side for medium, and 9 or more minutes to a side for well-done.
    To serve, place a fillet on a slice of eggplant, top with sauce and a thin slice of tomato. Dust with coarse ground black pepper and serve immediately.

Rib Eye Steaks with Seasoned Butters
GRILL-COOKED

For added flavor, top each tender rib eye steak with a pat of seasoned butter. See page 85 for flavored butters.

Have the rib eye (market) steaks cut about 1 inch thick. Barbecue about 5 inches from the heat for 4 to 6 minutes on each side for rare to medium doneness. Sprinkle with salt and pepper and serve, sizzling hot, topped with a ¼-inch pat of seasoned butter.

Honolulu Steak
GRILL-COOKED

This version of teriyaki steak from Honolulu may prove one of the finest flavor combinations you've tasted.

    6 rib eye steaks (also called market steaks)
        about 1 inch thick
    1 cup soy sauce
    1 clove garlic, crushed
    ¼ cup salad oil
    ¼ cup dry red wine
        Juice from small piece celery
        (about ¼ medium-sized stalk)

Arrange the steaks in a baking dish or bowl. Combine the soy sauce with the garlic, salad oil, wine, and celery juice. (Cut up the small piece of celery and put through the garlic press to obtain juice—a small but important part of this recipe.) Pour this marinade over the steaks and let stand for 30 minutes only. Remove from marinade, drain, and barbecue to doneness desired. Makes 6 servings.
    If you wish to use this same marinade on larger steaks, score the steaks lightly and marinate for 45 minutes to 1 hour, but no longer or the marinade flavors will be overpowering.

Steak au Poivre (Pepper Steak)
GRILL-COOKED

Hot, herb-scented tomato slices adorn this classic pepper steak. It gains flavor from barbecue smoke; then you flame it. Complete this menu with a Caesar salad, buttered crookneck squash, and a platter of fruit and cheese.

    2 teaspoons whole black peppers
    4 club steaks or small New York steaks,
        cut ¾ inch thick
    2 large tomatoes
    3 tablespoons butter or margarine
    ⅛ teaspoon sweet basil
    ⅛ teaspoon garlic salt
        Salt to taste
    4 tablespoons brandy

Crush whole black peppers coarsely with a mortar and pestle or rolling pin. Sprinkle both sides of the meat with the crushed peppers. Let meat stand at room temperature for at least 30 minutes to absorb flavor. Barbecue over hot coals (allow about 5 minutes on a side for rare). Transfer to a hot, heatproof serving platter. Slice the tomatoes ⅓ of an inch thick and sauté in melted butter in a frying pan, just until slices are hot through. Season with crumbled basil, garlic salt, and salt to taste. Arrange tomato slices on top of the steak. Warm brandy, ignite, and spoon flaming over the meat. Makes 4 servings.

Steak Kebabs
SKEWER-COOKED

Tender cubes of sirloin steak marinate in a flavorful wine-herb sauce. If you wish, carry the meat in its marinade to a picnic site, where it can then be skewered for barbecuing.

    ¾ cup dry red wine
    3 tablespoons olive oil
    3 tablespoons lemon juice
    2 cloves garlic, minced
    ½ teaspoon salt
    ¼ teaspoon rosemary
    ¼ teaspoon thyme
    3 pounds top sirloin steak,
        cut into 1½-inch cubes

To make the marinade, mix together the wine, olive oil, lemon juice, garlic, salt, rosemary, and thyme. Let meat marinate in this mixture for several hours or overnight, turning meat occasionally. Skewer the meat and barbecue over moderately hot coals, turning once, for about 8 minutes for rare meat. Makes 8 servings.

Whole Fillet with Blue-Cheese Log
GRILL-COOKED

For a really spectacular entrée, barbecue a whole fillet. It can be cooked right on the grill or on the spit. You can purchase the whole fillet (about 4 to 6 pounds) or a center cut fillet roast (about 2½ to 3 pounds). For a less expensive fillet barbecue, it is sometimes possible to get two tails of the fillet (the end portion of the tenderloin muscle which tapers toward the rib section) tied together securely; handle them as a whole fillet. If you plan to do this, place an order at your market ahead of time.

If you prepare the fillet on the grill, turn it quite often, exposing all sides to the heat. It's a lean cut, so brush frequently with a mixture of half melted butter and half oil. Or you may choose to have your meatman lard the fillet, wrapping a layer of fat around the meat so it self-bastes as it grills; this costs more, of course. It will take about 30 minutes to grill a whole fillet if you like it rare. Timing will be about the same when you spit roast.

For the most dramatic serving, place the charcoal-browned whole tenderloin on a handsome platter or board and garnish with the sprigs of watercress and a log of blue-cheese butter (recipe follows). Then carve generous, thick slices and serve as individual steaks. Place a pat of the butter on each serving of steak and let it melt.

To serve this superior meat to a large number of people, slice thin and offer as sandwiches on crusty buttered hot French bread. For a beautiful serving, cut a long thin loaf of French bread in half lengthwise. Spread cut surfaces generously with plain or seasoned butter. Heat. Arrange thin slices of the savory grilled steak on one half of the bread, thin slices of onions, tomatoes, and radishes or cucumbers on the other. Arrange the bread halves side by side, and cut diagonally across both to make 12 to 15 servings from a whole fillet.

Blue-Cheese Butter Log

    1 cup (2 cubes) soft butter
    ¼ pound blue cheese
    1 tablespoon finely chopped green onions,
        fresh rosemary, or basil
        Finely chopped parsley
        Watercress

Blend butter and cheese with onions, fresh rosemary, or basil. Place on a sheet of waxed paper, shape into a log, and roll in parsley. Wrap with waxed paper; refrigerate until firm. Serve on watercress.

Tournedos Héloïse
GRILL-COOKED

This is a prize steak entrée of many Western restaurants and one that benefits from barbecue cooking; the smoky flavor that permeates the meat as it grills over charcoal is excellent with the other choice ingredients.

Ask your meatman for tournedos, the small tenderloin steaks cut from the fillet. Visit a delicatessen or the gourmet section of your food store for the canned artichoke bottoms, pâté, and truffles.

½ pound small mushrooms, washed
2 tablespoons butter or margarine
   Salt and pepper to taste
1½ tablespoons lemon juice
¼ cup heavy cream
1 teaspoon cornstarch or arrowroot
6 artichoke bottoms, 3 inches in diameter
   (cooked or canned)
2 cans (4 oz. *each)* pâté de foie, chilled
6 beef tournedos, cut ¾ inch thick
   Truffles or ripe olives for garnish
   Madeira sauce (recipe follows)

Using a large frying pan, sauté mushrooms in melted butter. Season with salt and pepper to taste and sprinkle with lemon juice. Blend cream with cornstarch or arrowroot, and stir in; stirring constantly, cook until thickened. Set aside.

Heat artichoke bottoms in their own liquid. Open both ends of each can of pâté, and push out ¾ inch and slice; continue to slice the pâté, making 3 rounds from each can. Place pâté on foil, and heat in a 325° oven for 10 minutes.

Meanwhile, barbecue beef over hot coals (allowing about 2 to 3 minutes on a side for rare). Place artichoke bottoms at either end of a platter, top each with a hot tournedo, and arrange a slice of pâté and truffle on top.

Spoon Madeira sauce over (recipe follows), and arrange sautéed mushrooms in center of plate. Makes 6 servings.

Simple Madeira Sauce

Put 1 teaspoon beef extract in a small pan; add ¼ cup Madeira and simmer until slightly reduced. Blend ½ teaspoon cornstarch with 3 tablespoons water and stir in; cook until thickened.

Steak Sandwiches with Mushroom Sauce
GRILL-COOKED

Served on rye toast, these small steak sandwiches are covered with a red wine-mushroom sauce.

1½ pounds top sirloin, cut about ½ inch thick
   Red wine marinade (recipe follows)
   Salt
¾ pound mushrooms, sliced
3 tablespoons butter or margarine
6 slices light rye bread
   Chopped parsley

Cut sirloin into 6 equal-sized servings. Place meat in bowl; cover with red wine marinade (recipe follows). Cover and refrigerate for 1 to 2 hours. Drain meat, reserving marinade. Barbecue quickly to desired doneness; sprinkle lightly with salt. Keep steak warm while preparing sauce.

Sauté mushrooms in butter or margarine. Pour marinade into pan with mushrooms and cook quickly until reduced to sauce consistency. Toast bread. Place meat on toast; spoon sauce and mushrooms over each sandwich. Sprinkle with chopped parsley to garnish. Makes 6 servings.

Red Wine Marinade

½ cup dry red wine
½ medium-sized onion, cut in chunks
2 tablespoons lemon juice
¼ cup olive oil
1 clove garlic, sliced
½ teaspoon salt
   Dash pepper

Place in blender container the red wine, onion, lemon juice, olive oil, garlic, salt, and pepper; whirl until ingredients are well blended.

Sirloin à la Mirabeau
GRILL-COOKED

Latticed anchovy fillets and pimiento-stuffed olives make a decorative, flavorful topping for barbecued sirloin.

1 sirloin steak, cut 1½ inches thick
  (approximately 2½ lbs.)
1 tablespoon butter
1 teaspoon anchovy paste
  Freshly ground pepper
1 can (2 oz.) anchovy fillets
½ cup stuffed olives

Barbecue steak over hot coals for about 8 minutes. Turn, and spread the grilled side with butter blended with the anchovy paste. Barbecue the other side about 6 to 8 minutes, or to desired doneness. Remove to a carving board and season with pepper to taste. Arrange anchovy fillets, crisscross fashion, over the top, and fill each square with a sliced stuffed olive. Carve in 1-inch slices to serve. Make 4 servings.

Family Round Steak Barbecue
GRILL-COOKED

Ask your meatman to slice the first cut of the top round for this recipe; this is the tenderest portion of the round section, the part closest to the sirloin section.

If you buy high quality aged meat (such as U.S.D.A. graded choice beef), you won't need to tenderize this cut for the barbecue. If you're not sure of the meat's tenderness, however, it is a good idea to treat top round with meat tenderizer. The marinade also helps tenderize the steak.

First cut of top round (3 to 4 lbs.),
  cut 2 inches thick
⅓ cup wine vinegar
3 tablespoons salad oil
2 tablespoons honey (or use syrup from
  sweet pickles)
2 tablespoons chopped green onions
  with tops
1 clove garlic, minced or mashed
¼ teaspoon dried oregano or 1 teaspoon
  fresh oregano
¼ teaspoon dried rosemary or basil (or
  1 teaspoon of fresh rosemary or basil)
¾ teaspoon salt
¼ teaspoon paprika
  Butter
  Finely chopped parsley or watercress
  Avocado slices
  Lemon juice

Score both sides of top round on the diagonal, about ¼ inch deep. Marinate 4 to 5 hours or overnight in a mixture of the wine vinegar, salad oil, honey or syrup from sweet pickles, chopped green onions, garlic, oregano, rosemary or basil, salt, and paprika. Drain and save marinade. Grill over hot coals (about 10 to 12 minutes on each side for rare meat), basting with remaining marinade. As meat comes from the grill, place on slicing board, spread lightly with butter, and sprinkle with the chopped parsley or watercress. Arrange avocado slices, dipped in lemon juice, down center of steak. Slice across the grain. Makes 6 to 8 servings.

Oyster-Stuffed Market Steaks
GRILL-COOKED

For superlative steak, try stuffing market steaks with a luscious oyster and herb-flavored filling before they're grilled.

Have market steaks cut 1 inch thick. Slash horizontal pocket in inner curve of each of these slightly crescent-shaped steaks. Leave enough rim around outer edge of meat so filling won't break through. Lightly fill pocket with oyster stuffing (recipe below). Each steak will take ⅓ to ½ cup stuffing. Skewer edges together with strong toothpicks or little metal skewers. Grill over hot coals (about 5 minutes on each side for rare steak).

Oyster Stuffing

¼ cup finely sliced celery
2 tablespoons chopped onion
¼ cup (½ cube) butter or margarine
  Water, stock, or white wine
1 can (8 oz.) small oysters, drained,
  liquid reserved
½ package (8-oz. size) herb-seasoned
  stuffing mix
  Salt

Sauté sliced celery and chopped onion in butter or margarine until soft. Add water, stock, or white wine to oyster liquid to make ½ cup liquid. Add to sautéed celery and onions along with oysters, stuffing mix, and salt to taste. Mix lightly. Makes stuffing for 4 to 6 steaks.

Western Barbecue Steak

GRILL-COOKED

Try this barbecue treatment on any cut of beef. Bacon-onion overtones from a marinade-baste penetrate the steak.

    1 cup bacon drippings
    ½ cup finely chopped onions
    ⅓ cup lemon juice
    2 tablespoons catsup
    1 tablespoon Worcestershire
    1 tablespoon prepared horseradish
    1 teaspoon paprika
    ½ teaspoon salt
    ⅛ teaspoon pepper
    1 large clove garlic, minced or mashed
    2 bay leaves
    Steaks at least 1 inch thick for broiling
    (weight should total about 4 pounds)

Melt bacon drippings in a saucepan. Add chopped onions, lemon juice, catsup, Worcestershire, horseradish, paprika, salt, pepper, garlic, and bay leaves. Stir thoroughly. Place steaks in a single layer in a shallow pan. Pour sauce over meat. Allow to stand 30 minutes at room temperature. Turn steaks once during marinating time to be sure sauce reaches all surfaces of meat. Lightly grease barbecue grill. Drain excess marinade from steaks. Place on grill over hot barbecue coals. Broil on each side to your liking, basting with remaining marinade during grilling. Makes 6 generous servings.

Beefsteak Jalisco

GRILL-COOKED

You squeeze the juice of a fresh orange over this thick-cut barbecued top round steak. Since this recipe is Mexican in origin, you might serve it with your favorite cheese or sour cream enchiladas; a green salad with sliced onions, oranges, and cucumbers; and fresh fruit for dessert.

Have your meatman make the first cut of beef top round about 2 inches thick (this is the part next to the sirloin); you should have about 3 pounds or more.

Trim off all fat and gash the surface of the steak in a diagonal pattern, making ⅜-inch-deep cuts about 1 inch apart. Rub the meat lightly with salt. Grill about 5 to 6 inches over medium-hot coals for about 10 minutes on a side for rare meat; or cook to degree of doneness you prefer. Transfer meat to carving board and squeeze the juice of 1 cut orange over the meat. Slice meat vertically and make sure some of the accumulating juices moisten each piece. Makes 8 to 10 servings.

Porterhouse with Béarnaise

GRILL-COOKED

Here's a steak that's both good tasting and good looking; the meat is topped with sautéed mushrooms, and Béarnaise sauce in mushroom caps is served alongside.

    12 large mushrooms, approximately
        2½ inches in diameter, washed
    ½ pound small mushrooms, about
        ¾ inch in diameter, washed
    3 tablespoons butter or margarine
        Salt and pepper to taste
    1½ tablespoons lemon juice
    ¼ teaspoon crumbled dried tarragon
    2 large porterhouse steaks,
        cut 1½ inches thick
        Béarnaise sauce (recipe follows)
        Parsley

Remove stems from the large mushrooms and slice the stems. Leave small mushrooms whole. Melt the 3 tablespoons butter in a large frying pan and quickly sauté the large whole mushroom caps; season with salt and pepper to taste and remove from pan. Add the small whole mushrooms and the sliced stems to the pan; season with salt and pepper to taste and sprinkle with the lemon juice and crumbled tarragon. Sauté until mushrooms are just tender; set aside.

Grill steak to desired degree of doneness, allowing about 8 minutes to a side for rare, and place on a carving board. Surround with the large mushroom caps and spoon some Béarnaise sauce (recipe follows) into each one; garnish each filled mushroom cap with a parsley sprig. Spoon the sautéed small mushroom caps over grilled meat. Pass remaining sauce to spoon over the meat. Makes 4 to 6 servings.

Béarnaise Sauce

    1½ teaspoons crumbled dried tarragon
    1½ teaspoons chopped green onions or chives
    3 tablespoons white wine vinegar
    ½ cup (1 cube) butter
    3 egg yolks

Place tarragon and green onions or chives in a small saucepan. Add vinegar and cook until liquid is reduced by half. Heat butter until bubbly; reserve. Place egg yolks in a blender container (preheated with warm water), add the herb and vinegar mixture, and blend well. With the blender turned on, gradually pour in the melted butter in a steady stream and blend until smooth. Fill mushroom caps; spoon remaining sauce into serving bowl.

Grilled Eye of Round Steaks
GRILL-COOKED

These lean, firm-textured steaks require tenderizing before you barbecue them. Use an instant meat marinade (available in market meat departments) or your favorite meat marinade plus an unseasoned commercial meat tenderizer.

> Instant meat marinade or teriyaki marinade (recipe follows) plus unseasoned meat tenderizer
> 6 eye of round steaks, cut ½ inch thick
> Marinated or freshly cooked artichoke hearts for garnish

When using the instant meat marinade, follow package directions exactly. If you use another marinade, allow the meat to marinate for 1 to 2 hours; then use an unseasoned meat tenderizer as directed on the package.

Grill steaks 5 to 6 inches from heat for 3 to 4 minutes per side for medium doneness. Serve on a heated platter, garnished with marinated artichoke hearts and barbecued fruit or vegetables, if you wish. Makes 4 servings.

Teriyaki Marinade

> 1 cup beef broth
> ⅓ cup soy sauce
> 2 tablespoons lime juice
> 1 clove garlic, mashed
> 1 green onion with top, chopped
> 1 tablespoon firmly packed brown sugar

Combine the beef broth, soy sauce, lime juice, garlic, green onion, and brown sugar.

Steak with Roquefort Butter
GRILL-COOKED

The tangy chive-and-cheese spread melts into this steak and mixes with the meat juices.

> 1 flank steak (about 1½ lbs.)
> Well seasoned French-style dressing
> ¼ cup (½ cube) butter or margarine
> ½ cup Roquefort or blue cheese
> 1 clove garlic, minced
> 1 tablespoon chopped chives
> 2 tablespoons brandy

Marinate flank steak in your favorite well seasoned French-style dressing for several hours. For Roquefort butter, cream butter and cheese until blended; mix in garlic, chives, and brandy; turn into a bowl. (You may pre-

pare this ahead and refrigerate; warm to room temperature before using.)

Remove flank steak from marinade and barbecue over hot coals, allowing 5 minutes on each side for rare. Transfer to a hot platter and slice on the diagonal into ⅛-inch-thick slices. Spoon Roquefort butter over meat. Makes 4 servings.

Barbecued Beef Stroganoff
GRILL-COOKED

When midsummer barbecuing becomes a frequent family routine, it's sometimes a good idea to barbecue an extra quantity of meat for the next day. On an evening when you're having steaks, broil an extra piece of round steak so that you'll have smoke-flavored meat to make into Beef Stroganoff.

> 2 medium-sized onions, sliced, each slice cut in half
> 3 tablespoons butter
> 2 pounds barbecued round steak, cut into slices about 3 inches long, ½ inch wide
> ½ pound fresh mushrooms, sliced
> ½ cup regular strength beef broth (may be half dry wine)
> 2 cups commercial sour cream
> Salt
> Pepper
> Prepared mustard
> Hot steamed rice

Sauté onion slices in butter until wilted. Add the meat and mushrooms. Pour in beef broth and cover. Simmer until meat is tender and liquid has almost evaporated, about 40 minutes. Remove from heat and stir in sour cream. Season to taste with salt, pepper, and prepared mustard. Serve with hot steamed rice. Makes 6 servings.

Japanese-Style Steak
GRILL-COOKED

Choose top round, sirloin, or sirloin tip steaks for this mildly flavored variation of the classic teriyaki steak. If needed, tenderize it as directed on the package of meat tenderizer.

    2 pounds boneless beef steak,
       not more than 1 inch thick
    ¾ cup olive oil or other salad oil
    ½ cup wine vinegar
    1 large slice raw onion
    3 tablespoons soy sauce
    2 whole cloves
    2 bay leaves
       Juice of ½ medium-sized lemon
    ¼ teaspoon freshly ground black pepper
    3 tablespoons brown sugar

Remove the fat from the steaks and cut into serving-sized pieces. Combine the olive oil, wine vinegar, onion, soy sauce, cloves, bay leaves, lemon juice, pepper, and 1 tablespoon of the brown sugar. Pour over the steak and marinate at room temperature for about 1 hour; turn the steaks once. When you are ready to barbecue, remove steaks from the marinade and rub with the remaining 2 tablespoons brown sugar. Broil over charcoal until it is done to your liking. Makes 4 servings.

Garlic Steak in a Crust
GRILL-COOKED

Barbecue a steak inside a pastry crust and you get a tender, well-browned, extra-juicy steak. It's worth using the pastry wrap just to get such a good steak, but your eating audience will probably eat the crispy, near-charred pieces of the crust right along with the steak.

       Unseasoned meat tenderizer
       Boneless chuck steak, 1 inch thick,
          cut into 6 pieces each about 3 by 4 inches
       Salad oil
       Garlic salt
    4 cups all-purpose flour
    2 teaspoons salt
    1 cup shortening
       About ¾ cup cold water

Follow directions with unseasoned meat tenderizer to prepare steaks for cooking. Rub all sides of meat with salad oil; sprinkle generously with garlic salt.

   To make pastry, sift flour and measure; add salt. Cut in shortening and stir in cold water to make a soft dough. On lightly floured board, roll out dough about ⅛ inch thick. Cut into six ovals, each about 6 inches wide, 8 inches long. Place a piece of steak on one half of a pastry

oval; fold over pastry, moisten and seal edges together. Prick crust several times with a fork. Place steak turn-overs on grill above low coals. Cook about 45 minutes, turning to brown crust on all sides. Makes 6 servings.

Skirt Steak with Burgundy Sauce
GRILL-COOKED

Here is a recipe that calls for grilling rolled skirt steaks, then serving them with a special sauce of chopped chicken livers, mushrooms, onion, and Burgundy.

    6 rolled skirt steaks, secured with
       wooden picks
    1 small onion, chopped
    ¼ pound chicken livers, chopped
    1½ cups sliced fresh mushrooms, washed
    ¼ cup butter or margarine
    ½ teaspoon salt
       Dash freshly ground black pepper
    ⅓ cup Burgundy
       Parsley for garnish

Grill the steaks 5 to 6 inches from the source of heat for 7 to 9 minutes on each side. While the steaks are grilling, sauté the onion, chicken livers, and mushrooms in the butter until tender. Add the salt, pepper, and wine; boil rapidly for 3 to 4 minutes to reduce the liquid. To serve, arrange the steaks on a warm serving platter; pour the sauce over all and garnish with parsley. Makes 6 servings.

Teriyaki Steak Strips
GRILL-COOKED

These flank steak strips are exceptionally tender when you slice the steak diagonally, marinate it, then barbecue it quickly close to very hot coals just to the rare or medium-rare stage. You can lay the strips flat on the grill, string them on skewers, or place them in a hinged wire broiler.

  1 whole flank steak (about 1½ lbs.)
  1 cup undiluted beef consommé (use half
    dry red or dry white wine, if desired)
  ⅓ cup soy sauce
  1½ teaspoons seasoned salt
  ¼ cup chopped green onions with tops
  1 clove garlic, minced or mashed
  3 tablespoons lime juice
  2 tablespoons brown sugar or honey

Slice meat into ¼-inch-thick strips, cutting diagonally across the grain. Refrigerate overnight in a marinade made by combining the beef consommé, soy sauce, seasoned salt, green onions, garlic, lime juice, and brown sugar or honey. Drain meat and save marinade. Grill strips quickly over hot coals (about 2 minutes on each side), basting with marinade. Turn only once. Makes 5 or 6 servings.

Chef's Chuck Roast
GRILL-COOKED

When served, the chef's chuck roast will be charred outside, rare in the middle.

  2 cloves garlic, finely minced
  2 tablespoons olive oil
  ¼ teaspoon dry mustard
  1 teaspoon soy sauce
  ½ teaspoon rosemary, crushed, or
    1 sprig of the fresh herb
  2 tablespoons wine vinegar
  ¼ cup sauterne
    Chuck roast, 2½ to 3 inches thick
  2 tablespoons catsup
  ½ teaspoon Worcestershire
  1½ teaspoons meat seasoning sauce

Sauté garlic gently in olive oil, add mustard, soy sauce, and rosemary. Remove from fire and stir in vinegar and wine. Place roast in a bowl and pour sauce over it. During the next 24 hours, turn the meat frequently in the sauce.

To barbecue, remove the meat and to the remaining marinade add the catsup, Worcestershire, and meat seasoning sauce. Stir well and apply some of the mixture to meat before barbecuing; use as a basting sauce during cooking. If sauce appears too thick, add more olive oil.

The meat should be turned frequently and basted often. A piece of meat 2½ inches thick should be cooked over hot coals for 40 minutes to be charred outside and rare in the center. Makes 4 to 6 servings.

Barbecued Hanging Tenderloin
GRILL-COOKED

This tender piece of meat is similar to flank steak in size and coarseness of grain. It should be barbecued rapidly to your liking, then sliced on the diagonal in thin slices.

  1 hanging tenderloin (butcher steak),
    about 2 pounds
  ¼ cup olive oil
  1½ tablespoons wine vinegar
  2 cloves garlic, minced or mashed
  1 teaspoon rosemary
  ¼ teaspoon salt
  ¼ teaspoon pepper

Brush hanging tenderloin with a mixture of olive oil, wine vinegar, garlic, rosemary, salt, and pepper. Allow steak to marinate for 1 hour. Basting with remaining marinade, barbecue steak over hot coals to your liking (about 8 minutes on each side for rare). Turn only once. Slice across the grain, on the diagonal from the top to the bottom of the steak. Makes 5 or 6 servings.

Skirt Steaks Teriyaki
GRILL-COOKED

Many meat markets sell skirt steaks rolled jelly-roll fashion and fastened with wooden skewers. Two of these pinwheels are made from each skirt steak.

  1 teaspoon unseasoned meat tenderizer
  6 or 8 skirt steak pinwheels
  ¼ cup Sherry
  ¼ cup soy sauce
  ¼ teaspoon ground ginger
  ¼ teaspoon garlic powder
    Dash pepper

Rub tenderizer into both sides of each steak; place in a shallow container that can be tightly covered. Combine Sherry, soy sauce, ginger, garlic powder, and pepper; pour over meat. Cover and chill for several hours or overnight; turn once or more, if possible. Barbecue for 6 to 8 minutes on each side, or until steaks are well browned. Makes 6 to 8 servings.

steak with a thin slice of natural jack cheese and a slice of tomato. When brown on the under side, lift steak to a hot crusty buttered bun or slice of French bread to serve.

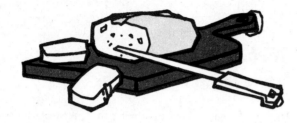

Chuck Steak with Anchovy Butter
GRILL-COOKED

At serving time, each guest tops his serving of grilled steak with a slice of lemon-anchovy butter cut from a butter ring garnish.

1 chuck steak, cut 1 inch thick
   Unseasoned meat tenderizer
   Lemon-anchovy butter (recipe follows)

Prepare chuck steak with unseasoned meat tenderizer according to package instructions. Grill over hot coals until done to the stage you prefer (about 5 minutes on each side for rare). Cut into serving portions and serve immediately, topped with lemon-anchovy butter.

Lemon-Anchovy Butter Ring

Combine ½ cup (1 cube) soft butter, 1 teaspoon lemon juice, and 1 can (2 oz.) anchovy fillets. Press into small ring mold (about 3 inches across), oiled and sprinkled with finely chopped parsley. Chill until firm. At serving time, dip into warm water and unmold on a bed of parsley. Makes enough butter to top 6 to 8 steak servings.

Pizza-Style Cube Steaks
GRILL-COOKED

Have sirloin tip steaks cut thick enough so that when they're run through the tenderizer to make cube steaks, they'll be a bit less than ½ inch thick. Each steak should weigh not less than 6 ounces; plan on one per person.

Brush steaks with a mixture of half salad oil and half lemon juice. Broil quickly on one side, very close to hot coals. Turn and sprinkle browned side with dill weed, oregano, rosemary, or a favorite herb blend. Top each

Crunchy Onion-Beef Burgers
GRILL-COOKED

Canned fried onions add crunchy texture and robust onion flavor to the grilled meat.

1½ pounds lean ground beef or ground chuck
1½ teaspoons salt
  ⅛ teaspoon pepper
  1 tablespoon catsup
  1 can (3½ oz.) French-fried onions
  6 hamburger buns or English muffins, split
    Butter

In a bowl combine meat, salt, pepper, and catsup; mix until well blended. Add half of the can of French-fried onions to the meat mixture; use a fork to gently mix the onions with the meat. Shape the meat into 6 patties, about ½ inch thick. Barbecue the patties as rare or as well done as you prefer. Sprinkle remaining French-fried onions over tops of the meat patties after they are cooked. Or pass a bowl of the remaining onions along with relishes at the table. Serve inside the hamburger buns or English muffins, which have been lightly toasted and buttered. Makes 6 sandwiches.

Cheeseburgers with Guacamole
GRILL-COOKED

Guacamole topping gives these broiled cheeseburgers a Mexican flavor. You might serve these with a mixed green salad, green beans, toasted French rolls, fresh apples, and brownies for an easy family supper.

Mix together 1½ pounds lean ground chuck, ½ teaspoon salt, ½ teaspoon garlic salt, ½ teaspoon onion salt, and 1 teaspoon Worcestershire. Mix in 1½ cups shredded sharp Cheddar cheese. Shape into 4 patties, 1 inch thick. Grill over hot coals 3 to 4 minutes on a side for rare meat. Top with guacamole sauce, made by blending 1 can (7¾ oz.) thawed frozen avocado dip (guacamole) with 1 tablespoon lemon juice and 3 drops liquid hot-pepper seasoning. (Or substitute 1 fresh avocado, peeled and mashed, for the frozen dip.) Makes 4 servings.

Hamburger Steak in the Round
GRILL-COOKED

Rich meat juices mingle with a mustard and chile-seasoned butter, then sink into the French bread as you grill these giant hamburgers over hot coals.

1 round loaf French bread,
    cut in half horizontally
½ cup (1 cube) soft butter
½ teaspoon prepared mustard
½ teaspoon chile powder
3 pounds ground beef chuck
2 teaspoons seasoned salt
½ cup finely chopped green onions with tops
2 tablespoons chile sauce
1 tablespoon soy sauce or Worcestershire
    Thin cucumber half-slices
    Small tomato half-slices

Spread cut surfaces of French bread with seasoned barbecue butter made by blending the soft butter, mustard, and chile powder.

Combine ground chuck with seasoned salt, chopped green onions, chile sauce, and soy sauce or Worcestershire. Shape into 2 round patties each a little larger than the bread (the meat shrinks slightly when cooked). Place bread, crust side down, at back of grill (away from hottest coals) to heat slowly. Barbecue meat patties on one side until browned and partially done. Turn patties, and place bread, buttered side down, on top of them. Continue grilling patties until undersides are browned and meat is cooked to degree desired.

To serve, turn meat and bread onto serving platter with bread on bottom, meat on top. Garnish with alternating cucumber and tomato half-slices on top of meat patties, marking individual portions. Cut each round into wedges to make 10 to 12 servings.

Beef and Cheese Stacks
GRILL-COOKED

Fit these ground beef and cheese stacks between split toasted buns for a husky sandwich or serve the stacks without buns, if you wish.

2 pounds lean ground beef
2 tablespoons minced dried onions
2 teaspoons Worcestershire
2 teaspoons prepared mustard
1 teaspoon salt
½ teaspoon pepper
1½ cups shredded sharp Cheddar cheese
    Melted butter

Thoroughly mix together the ground beef, onions, Worcestershire, mustard, salt, and pepper. Divide into 12 portions, and form each into a thin patty. Put ¼ cup cheese in a mound on top of each of 6 of the patties; top each with another meat patty and press edges together to seal. Grill over hot coals to your liking (about 5 minutes on each side for medium). Baste with melted butter; turn only once. Makes 6 servings.

Stretched Hamburger
GRILL-COOKED

One pound of ground beef will make 8 hamburgers when prepared according to this recipe.

1 pound ground beef
2 carrots, grated
2 stalks celery, finely chopped
1 sprig parsley, finely chopped
1 green pepper, finely chopped
1 onion, finely chopped
1 clove garlic, finely chopped
1 tablespoon steak sauce
1 egg
    Dash salt and pepper
2 tablespoons cooking oil or shortening
8 hamburger buns
½ cup (1 cube) melted butter or margarine
8 large tomato slices
    Sliced unpeeled cucumber

Mix together the ground beef, carrots, celery, parsley, green pepper, onion, garlic, steak sauce, egg, salt, pepper, and oil. Roll into patties the size of the hamburger buns and grill. Split hamburger buns into halves and toast cut sides; then brush with melted butter. Cover each hamburger with one slice of tomato and several slices of fresh, crisp, unpeeled cucumber. A little prepared mustard may be added, if desired. Makes 8 servings.

Soy-Dipped Hamburgers
GRILL-COOKED

You can shape these hamburgers and place them in their marinade (tightly covered) just before leaving home for a family picnic. Take along a small hibachi, or use a deep cake pan and cake rack for grilling the hamburgers. You might complete a picnic menu with a marinated bean salad, fresh fruit, and beverages.

½ cup soy sauce
½ cup water
1 clove garlic, crushed
2 teaspoons grated fresh ginger
2 tablespoons Worcestershire
6 tablespoons brown sugar
3 pounds lean ground beef
8 sourdough French rolls
   Thinly sliced tomatoes
   Sliced green pepper

Combine soy sauce, water, garlic, ginger, Worcestershire, and brown sugar. Shape ground beef into 8 log-shaped meat patties (to fit the long French bread rolls). Pour marinade over the meat, cover, and marinate for 1 to 1½ hours. Cook meat over hot coals until done to your liking. Split and toast rolls on the grill and fill with the meat patties, thinly sliced tomatoes, and sliced green pepper. Makes 8 servings.

Marinated Beef Shortribs
GRILL-COOKED

After these shortribs have been marinated, the marinade is used to make two sauces, one for basting the meat, and another to serve with the meat.

6 pounds beef shortribs, cut about
   3 inches long
2½ cups tomato juice
1 tablespoon sugar
1 teaspoon Worcestershire
¼ teaspoon ginger
¼ teaspoon allspice
1 teaspoon celery salt
½ cup vinegar
1 onion, finely chopped
1 clove garlic, cut
   Basting sauce (recipe follows)
   Serving sauce (recipe follows)

Marinate the meat for 48 hours in a mixture of the tomato juice, sugar, Worcestershire, ginger, allspice, celery salt, and vinegar. Place in the refrigerator and turn the meat frequently. For the last 4 hours, remove from the refrigerator and add the chopped onion and garlic.

Remove the meat from the marinade and put in a Dutch oven with a little water. Cover and cook over low heat. When almost tender, take out and complete cooking on the barbecue grill. Baste with basting sauce (recipe follows) until brown and slightly crisp. Serve with serving sauce (recipe follows). Makes 8 servings.

Basting Sauce

While meat is cooking, strain marinade; discard onion and garlic. Mix ½ cup of marinade with ¼ cup of olive oil or drippings. Baste the meat with this mixture while barbecuing.

Serving Sauce

Use the rest of the marinade to make the following sauce to serve with the meat. Sauté a finely chopped onion until brown; add the marinade, 1 teaspoon powdered oregano, and 1 teaspoon cumin. (If these are not available, substitute 2 teaspoons chile powder.) Boil the sauce down until it is about half the original volume.

Barbecued Rib Bones
GRILL-COOKED

Purchase about 6 pounds meaty rib bones (about 16 ribs) and let stand several hours or overnight in your favorite barbecue sauce or oil-vinegar marinade, turning occasionally to coat the bones and meat evenly.

To barbecue the bones, drain and place over medium-hot coals (about 5 inches from heat), bone side up. Turn ribs to brown on all sides, basting with the sauce or marinade. Cook a total of approximately 20 minutes. Makes about 6 servings.

Chef's Ground Beef
GRILL-COOKED

For unqualified success, make certain that those on the receiving end of this loaf like rare meat, and that the sauce is ready before the meat is put on the flames.

1½ pounds ground lean beef
  1 teaspoon salt
¼ teaspoon pepper
  2 tablespoons butter or margarine

Blend the ground beef, salt, and pepper, and form into a loaf about 3 inches wide and 1½ inches thick. Spread the butter over the loaf.

Broil meat over coals, lowering grill so that the meat is close to the coals. (Extinguish serious flareups immediately.) Count on 5 to 6 minutes for each side, carefully turning the meat only once with a broad spatula. The result should be a loaf crusty brown on the outside, deliciously rare inside.

Place the loaf on a sizzling hot platter the instant it comes from the fire, and pour over it the lemon-butter sauce (recipe follows). Slice into individual servings and serve on warm plates without further delay. Makes 3 or 4 servings.

Lemon-Butter Sauce

1 tablespoon butter or margarine
1 tablespoon chopped parsley
1 tablespoon lemon juice
⅛ teaspoon salt
  Pepper
  Paprika

Melt butter, and add parsley, lemon juice, salt, and a sprinkling of paprika and pepper.

Rosemary Barbecued Sirloin
SMOKE-COOKED

This steak is a simple one to serve for a barbecue gathering of several families.

2 tablespoons fresh rosemary or
  2 teaspoons dried rosemary
1 boneless top sirloin steak,
  cut 2 inches thick (about 4½ lbs.)
  Salt
  Pepper

Press rosemary into the meat, coating both sides. Place over medium barbecue coals and cover with barbecue hood (if barbecue doesn't have a hood, make one with heavy aluminum foil as directed on page 14). Barbecue about 15 minutes on each side for rare meat, or until the meat thermometer registers 135° for rare. (You can insert a meat thermometer into meat after barbecuing one side.) Place on a carving board and season with salt and pepper; then slice on the diagonal. Makes 10 to 12 servings.

Mushroom-Filled Hamburger Cups
GRILL-COOKED

You can make these individual hamburger cups by molding ground beef over the bottoms of foil muffin cups. Then barbecue them over hot coals and fill with mushrooms and cheese. Serve with corn on the cob, green salad, and sourdough French bread.

To shape the cups, buy foil muffin pans. Use kitchen shears to cut the muffin cups apart; trim the edges of each cup to make it round.

1½ pounds ground chuck
  1 egg
  3 tablespoons fine dry bread crumbs
½ teaspoon salt
¼ teaspoon pepper
  Sautéed mushrooms (recipe follows)
  About ½ cup shredded Cheddar cheese

Mix together ground chuck, egg, bread crumbs, salt, and pepper. Divide meat mixture into 6 equal portions, forming each portion into a patty about ½ inch thick and 4 inches in diameter. Mold each patty evenly over the bottom of a foil muffin cup. Place on grill, with the inside of the muffin cup facing down.

Cook until bottom edges are browned and the top part of the mound is still slightly pink. (Meat next to cup should be cooked enough that it will hold its cup shape when turned.) Turn; remove foil cups carefully. Fill meat cups with sautéed mushrooms (recipe follows); top each with about 1 tablespoon cheese. Return to barbecue and cook only until cheese melts. Makes 6 servings.

Sautéed Mushrooms

2 tablespoons butter or margarine
1 tablespoon chopped green onion
1 tablespoon chopped parsley
½ pound mushrooms, quartered
¼ teaspoon salt
⅛ teaspoon pepper

In a small pan, melt butter or margarine, add green onion, parsley, mushrooms, salt, and pepper. Cook slowly until mushrooms are tender, stirring occasionally.

Herbed Beef Shanks with Summer Squash

GRILL-COOKED

As a slight departure from usual barbecuing, you might like to grill precooked beef shanks, coated lightly with seasoned crumbs, along with colorful sections of summer squash.

4 slices meaty beef shank,
    each cut 1 inch thick
2 cups water
½ medium-sized onion, sliced
1 carrot, sliced
1 bay leaf
8 whole black peppers
1 teaspoon salt
6 tablespoons butter or margarine
½ teaspoon basil
2 teaspoons prepared mustard
½ teaspoon prepared horseradish
½ to ¾ cup fine dry bread crumbs
4 medium-sized crookneck or zucchini
    squash, cut in half lengthwise
    Salt
    Prepared mustard

First cook the beef shanks: Place them in a wide shallow pan. Add water, onion, carrot, bay leaf, whole black peppers, and salt. Bring to a boil, cover, and simmer very slowly for about 1½ hours or until tender. Let cool slightly in stock, then gently remove shanks (save stock for soup) and cut away the bone.

Melt butter or margarine; blend in basil, mustard, and horseradish. Dip meat in butter mixture, then coat with fine dry bread crumbs. Dip squash in the butter mixture. Sprinkle with salt.

Place vegetables, cut side down, and beef on a grill about 5 to 6 inches above medium-hot coals. Cook about 10 minutes, turning as needed, or until meat is brown and squash is tender and brown. Brush squash with the butter; it may take a little longer (up to 15 minutes) to cook. Pour remaining butter over meat and vegetables before serving. Pass additional mustard to eat with the hot beef. Makes 4 servings.

Steak on the Coals

COAL-COOKED

For dramatic effect and delicious meat, try cooking a steak right on the coals. You have to practice it a time or two before you can count on reasonably consistent results. It's so much fun, though, that you'll probably consider it worth the risk.

Build up your fire until you have about 2 to 3 inches of coals. Use a hard charcoal or hardwood that gives off a very fine ash after it burns. It is a good idea to whisk any surplus ash off the top of the coals with a brush or blow it off with a bellows.

Use any good steak, cut 1 to 1½ inches thick. Have steak at room temperature and throw it directly on the coals. Turn it when the juices show on top and place on an area of coals not previously covered by the steak. Actually the steak doesn't burn; it damps down the fire a bit, unless you get your bed of coals too thick and hot. The cooking process should take about 10 to 15 minutes.

Cumin Steak Strips and Cheese

SMOKE-COOKED

Thin slices of smoked flank steak and Muenster cheese are layered on warm bread for hot open sandwiches.

1 flank steak (about 1½ lbs.)
    Hot bread slices
½ pound Muenster cheese, sliced thin
    Powdered cumin

Place flank steak on grill over very hot coals; cover with a hood or foil and grill 5 minutes on each side. Place on carving board and slice very thinly, on the diagonal. Arrange hot steak strips on top of hot bread slices as an open sandwich, alternating and overlapping steak with thin slices of Muenster cheese. Sprinkle with powdered cumin. Makes 4 servings.

Top Round Steak with Artichoke Hearts
SMOKE-COOKED

Marinated artichoke hearts season and garnish this thick-cut top round steak. Ask your meatman to cut a 2-inch-thick steak off the top of the round. Depending on the size of the animal, you will have 3 to 5 or more pounds of solid lean meat. Best results can be obtained on a covered barbecue. You can use a meat thermometer to ensure having it done just the way you like it.

If you wish, use unseasoned meat tenderizer (follow package directions). Drain the marinade from 1 jar (6 oz.) marinated artichoke hearts into a measuring cup; add salad oil if needed to make ¼ cup (reserve artichokes). Add ½ cup dry red wine. Trim fat from steak and put meat in a baking dish; pour over the marinade; let stand about 1 hour.

Lift out the meat (reserving the marinade), and place on the grill over low bed of coals. Cover the barbecue with a hood and cook slowly. When well browned on one side, about 25 to 30 minutes, turn steak over and baste with reserved marinade. Insert a meat thermometer, if you have one, into the center of the meat. Also arrange the reserved artichoke hearts on top. Cover the barbecue again and continue cooking until done. (If you like meat quite rare, remove this cut from grill at 135°.) The total time required to cook a 4-pound steak rare is about 35 minutes. Slice diagonally across the grain to serve. A 4-pound steak makes about 8 servings.

Korean Shortrib Barbecue
GRILL-COOKED

Barbecued shortribs, Korean style, make good eating for a picnic. You charcoal-grill these meaty pieces of beef to a crusty brown and eat them with your fingers like chicken.

A special way of cutting shortribs and a savory marinade distinguish the Korean barbecue. When you buy the shortribs, ask your meatman to saw through the bone at 2½-inch intervals so you can dice-cut the meat chunks as directed below.

4 pounds well trimmed beef shortribs,
    sawed through bone at 2½-inch intervals
½ cup soy sauce
½ cup water
¼ cup sliced green onions with tops
2 tablespoons sesame seed
2 tablespoons sugar
2 cloves garlic, minced or mashed
½ teaspoon pepper

With bone side down, dice-cut the 2½-inch shortrib cubes as follows: Cut meat halfway to bone every ½ inch in one direction; at right angles, cut every ½ inch, but go only ½ inch deep. To make marinade, combine the soy sauce, water, onions, sesame seed, sugar, garlic, and pepper. Put scored pieces of meat into marinade and chill, covered, in refrigerator for 4 to 5 hours.

Place meat, bone side down, on barbecue grill over high heat. When brown, turn and cook on meat side. Lift and turn meat throughout cooking time (about 15 minutes) to expose all surfaces to heat. Cook until crisply browned and done to your preference. Have plenty of napkins on hand and eat while hot. Makes 4 servings.

Oyster-Topped Beef Fillet
SMOKE-COOKED

A slice of onion, a slice of lemon, and a large smoked oyster top each of these juicy fillets.

Grill 1½-inch-thick beef fillet steaks (1 for each serving) over charcoal fire (allow 5 minutes on each side for rare steaks; sear 1 minute on each side, then cover with a hood or foil to finish smoke-cooking). Place thin crosswise slices of onion, thin crosswise slices of lemon, and drained large oysters (one each per serving) on a sheet of heavy foil. Brush with melted butter. Place on grill to heat and smoke as steaks cook. Stack on each steak an onion slice, a lemon slice, and a smoked oyster; grind black pepper over top.

Smoked Sirloin Tip
SMOKE-COOKED

If you have a Chinese smoke oven, fire it up and try this recipe for smoked sirloin tip.

    3 to 4 pounds sirloin tip,
        cut in 1¼-inch-thick slices

Marinade

    4 tablespoons salad oil
    2 tablespoons paprika
    1½ teaspoons salt
    ¼ teaspoon coarsely ground pepper
    1½ teaspoons onion salt
    ¼ teaspoon garlic salt
    1 tablespoon soy sauce
    ½ teaspoon whole oregano, crumbled
    ½ teaspoon liquid hot-pepper seasoning
        (or less, to taste)
    2 tablespoons white port wine
    ½ teaspoon dry mustard

Combine marinade ingredients and marinate steaks about 2 hours, turning occasionally. Hang from top of smoke oven. Cook about 11 minutes at 450° — or longer as necessary, depending on the efficiency of your oven. Steaks will be a little on the rare side. Makes 6 to 8 servings.

Pizza-Flavored Meat Loaf
GRILL-COOKED

Cheese strips melt on top of this meat loaf that's cooked in a 9-inch foil pan on the grill of a covered barbecue.

    2 medium-sized onions, finely chopped
    3 tablespoons olive oil or salad oil
    1 large can (6 or 8 oz.) sliced mushrooms,
        drained
    2 eggs
    1½ cups soft bread crumbs
    1 can (10½ oz.) pizza sauce
    ½ cup chopped parsley
    1 teaspoon dried whole basil
    ¾ teaspoon salt
    ⅛ teaspoon pepper
    2 pounds ground beef chuck
    2 slices jack cheese, cut in strips

Sauté onions in oil until soft and lightly browned; add mushrooms and cook for about 3 minutes longer. Beat eggs slightly; blend in bread crumbs. Measure ¼ cup of the pizza sauce; reserve it for basting. Add remaining pizza sauce, parsley, basil, salt, pepper, onion mixture, and ground beef to egg mixture; mix lightly. Pat meat mixture into a 9-inch foil pie pan placed inside another foil pan, to give double thickness.

Place pan on grill above glowing coals (coals should be arranged in a circle around edge of barbecue, or at sides, so meat isn't directly over fire). Cover barbecue, and cook loaf for 45 minutes, adjusting drafts so fire burns slowly. Brush surface of meat with reserved pizza sauce, cover again, and continue cooking for 15 to 30 minutes longer until meat in center reaches preferred doneness (insert a small knife to test). Arrange cheese strips on top, and cover again until cheese melts. Cut in wedges and serve directly from pan. (Or you can cut edges of foil pan in several places with kitchen scissors; flatten pan edge. Using 2 broad spatulas, place loaf on a warm serving plate.) Makes 6 to 8 servings.

Lazy Holiday Roast
SPIT-ROASTED

Once the marinade for this cross-rib roast is made, you're ready to enjoy a leisurely holiday. Marinate the meat overnight and, when the day of celebration dawns, just put the roast over the fire and sit back until time to carve.

    1 boneless beef cross-rib roast (4 to 5 lbs.),
        rolled and tied
    ⅓ cup catsup
    ¾ cup dry red wine (or ½ cup water and
        ¼ cup red wine vinegar)
    ½ cup salad oil
    1 tablespoon instant minced onion
    1 tablespoon Worcestershire
    1 teaspoon crumbled rosemary
    1½ teaspoons salt
    ¼ teaspoon pepper
    5 drops liquid smoke seasoning (optional)

Set roast in a deep, close fitting bowl. Blend together catsup, wine (or water and red wine vinegar), salad oil, instant minced onion, Worcestershire, crumbled rosemary, salt, pepper, and liquid smoke seasoning. Pour this mixture over the roast; if it does not cover meat, turn roast over several times while marinating. Cover and refrigerate 12 to 24 hours. Lift meat from marinade and insert a meat thermometer into the center.

Cook roast on a rotisserie or in a covered barbecue, basting frequently with marinade. On a rotisserie, place meat 6 inches above medium-hot coals; in covered barbecue have medium coals. Both methods of cooking require about 1½ hours for rare to medium-rare meat. The meat thermometer should register 130° for rare or 140° for medium-rare to medium. (This is lower than most recommendations for beef, but because the cross-rib is so lean, the lower temperature is better.) Let roast stand about 20 minutes, then slice thinly and serve with meat juices. Makes 8 to 10 servings.

Savory Chuck Roast

GRILL-COOKED

The sauce for this chuck roast may be used either hot or cold. It keeps well in the refrigerator and may also be frozen for use later.

    5-pound chuck roast, cut about 2 inches thick
    Unseasoned meat tenderizer

Sauce
    1 onion
    4 tablespoons olive oil
    1 clove garlic, chopped
    ½ cup finely sliced celery
    ¾ cup chile sauce
    ¾ cup catsup
    ½ cup water
    2 tablespoons Worcestershire
    2 tablespoons wine vinegar
    1 teaspoon horseradish
    1 teaspoon prepared mustard
    2 tablespoons lemon juice
    2 teaspoons hickory smoked salt
    Liquid hot-pepper seasoning to taste
    ½ teaspoon freshly ground black pepper
    3 tablespoons brown sugar, firmly packed
    ½ cup Sherry or white or dry red wine

Treat meat with tenderizer according to package directions. Slice onion finely and break into rings. Put olive oil in skillet; add chopped garlic and the onion; sauté until onion is golden brown. Blend in celery, chile sauce, catsup, water, Worcestershire, vinegar, horseradish, mustard, lemon juice, smoked salt, liquid hot pepper, black pepper, and sugar. Bring to a boil and continue simmering slowly for 20 minutes. Add wine, increasing amount if necessary, so the mixture will have a moderately thick consistency and will be just right for applying with a brush. Simmer for an additional 10 minutes.

With the sauce, thoroughly baste the tenderized chuck roast. Place roast on grill close to a hot barbecue fire and brown on both sides. Then raise the grill so the roast will get only moderate heat; cover and cook until done (1 to 2 hours, depending on heat of fire and degree of rareness you wish), turning once. Baste very frequently. Cut in thin slices across the grain. Makes 4 to 6 servings.

Making Beef Jerky on the Barbecue

GRILL-COOKED

If family and friends enjoy the chewiness of good beef jerky, you can make it for them right on your barbecue grill. Besides the barbecue, the only things you need are:

a piece of light-weight screen to keep flies off the meat, a cover for the grill to keep out moisture at night, 3 or 4 days of warm summer sun, and very lean beef.

Preparing Meat for Jerky. When making a batch of jerky, start with a minimum of 3 to 5 pounds of very lean beef; this will yield less than 1 pound of jerky. Round steak, flank steak, or other very lean beef will make good jerky. Have your meatman cut the beef into steaks about 1½ inches thick. Then trim away all the fat (this is important because the fat can become rancid) and cut the meat into strips ⅛ to ¼-inch wide. Make the strips as long as possible.

The seasoning of beef jerky is entirely a matter of taste. If the meat is to be used on a hiking or camping trip, you'll want to leave it unseasoned or simply sprinkle both sides lightly with salt and pepper. (Eating salty jerky on a hike may make you thirsty.) For appetizers, make the jerky more highly seasoned.

Appetizer Jerky. To make jerky for appetizers or snacks, soak meat in the following marinade:

Combine 1 tablespoon onion powder, 1 tablespoon seasoned salt, 1 teaspoon garlic powder, 1 teaspoon black pepper, ½ cup Worcestershire, and ½ cup soy sauce. Pour this mixture over the strips of meat, mix gently, and let stand in the refrigerator several hours or overnight, stirring occasionally. Then drain the meat and dry as suggested.

Drying the Meat. For drying the meat, your barbecue grill should be as clean as possible. It is a good idea to line the bottom (the charcoal box) with foil, shiny side up, so the bottom is clean in case any meat falls into it. This also increases the reflection from the sun. Place the grill on the barbecue about 2 inches below top. Place the lightly seasoned, unseasoned, or marinated and drained meat across the grids: Do not let the strips overlap or touch each other. Then fasten a canopy of light-weight screen over the barbecue to keep out flies, bugs, and leaves (do not let the canopy touch the meat).

Put the meat out to dry in the morning. When the sun goes down you'll want to cover the barbecue or put it under a shelter to keep the meat from absorbing any moisture from the air. The meat will dry on one side in 1 to 2 days, depending on the heat of the sun and the dryness of the air. Turn the meat and let it dry another 1 to 2 days. When the jerky is dry and ready to eat, it is rather brittle and chewy. You can serve it immediately or store it in a covered container (or wrapped in foil or plastic film) in a dry place.

LAMB

For centuries lamb has been a favorite barbecue meat because it is generally tender and cooks well by this dry heat method.

Cook lamb as you would beef, preferably medium-rare for most tastes; that is, it should be crusty brown outside, delicately pink and juicy within.

For lamb cooked to the medium-rare stage, a properly placed meat thermometer will read about 150°. Medium doneness is about 160°, and more well done meat will have an internal temperature of about 170°.

The cooks of many countries favor lamb, and the recipes in this section reflect this international popularity. The Greeks favor lemon, oregano, and olive oil with lamb. In India or Pakistan the spices are sweeter and hotter—coriander, cumin, cinnamon, chiles. The Turks enjoy mint with lamb, and garlic is a favorite everywhere.

Russian Shashlik
SKEWER-COOKED

Pomegranate juice is the unusual ingredient in the tart, fruit-flavored marinade for these Russian-style lamb kebabs. Use an orange juicer to ream the pomegranate halves. Put the juicer in the sink to protect yourself from the spattering juice; wear an apron and rubber gloves. A complete Russian-American dinner menu featuring these kebabs might also include fried eggplant slices; rice pilaf; breadsticks; salad of sliced tomatoes, onions, and green pepper; with sherbet for dessert.

1 whole pomegranate, halved
1 lemon
½ cup chopped onion
¼ cup salad oil
½ teaspoon salt
   Dash pepper
2 pounds boneless lean lamb (leg or shoulder meat), cut in 1½-inch cubes
2 tablespoons chopped fresh onion
   Lemon slices
   Parsley

Ream the pomegranate to make about ½ cup juice; then ream the lemon to make about 3 tablespoons juice. Combine with the ½ cup chopped onion, salad oil, salt, and pepper. Pour this marinade over lamb cubes. Stir gently to coat the meat with the marinade. Cover and refrigerate the meat several hours or overnight.

Then drain meat and string on skewers. Broil or barbecue about 5 minutes on each side, turning skewers once. Arrange the lamb on a serving platter and sprinkle with the 2 tablespoons chopped fresh onion. Garnish with lemon slices and parsley, if you wish. Makes 4 to 6 servings.

Lamb Leg Chops
GRILL-COOKED

From one leg of lamb, a family of four can have two dinners: the large lamb chops or steaks featured in this recipe, then stew or kebabs made from the remaining shank end of the leg.

4 lamb leg chops or steaks,
   cut ¾ to 1 inch thick
⅔ cup salad oil
⅓ cup lemon juice
1 medium-sized onion, chopped
1 teaspoon salt
1 teaspoon oregano
   Dash pepper
   Parsley sprigs
   Lemon slices
   Onion slices

Marinate leg chops in salad oil, lemon juice, onion, salt, oregano, and pepper at least 4 hours. Drain chops. Grill over hot coals about 6 minutes on each side, or until done. Baste with marinade. Garnish with parsley, lemon and onion slices. Makes 4 to 6 servings, depending on size of chops.

Basic Lamb Sauce

This simple sauce adds flavor to any cut of lamb.

¾ cup Sherry
1 slice lemon
1 sprig parsley, minced
2 tablespoons olive oil
1 teaspoon grated onion
1 teaspoon salt
½ teaspoon pepper
1 sprig fresh rosemary, minced,
   or ½ teaspoon dried rosemary
1 sprig fresh oregano, minced,
   or ½ teaspoon dried oregano

Mix ingredients and let stand for several hours to allow flavors to blend.

Butterflied Leg of Lamb with Herb Baste
GRILL-COOKED

If you have a leg of lamb "butterflied" (boned, with the seam left open), you have a fine piece of meat to barbecue flat on the grill. In less than an hour, it cooks to a rich brown outside, with thin portions of the meat well-done and the thick portions slightly pink. There's no bone to deal with in carving, and you can offer well-done and rare slices.

This recipe may seem overloaded with herbs, but the barbecuing process chars them slightly, until they add a distinctive toasty flavor.

1 cup dry red or white wine
¾ cup regular strength chicken or beef broth
2½ tablespoons orange marmalade
2 tablespoons wine vinegar
1 tablespoon minced dried onion
1 tablespoon dried or fresh rosemary
1 tablespoon dried whole marjoram
1 large bay leaf, crumbled
1 teaspoon seasoned salt
¼ teaspoon powdered ginger
1 leg of lamb (5 to 6 lbs.),
   boned and butterflied

Combine in a pan the wine, chicken or beef stock, orange marmalade, and wine vinegar. Stir in onion, rosemary, marjoram, bay leaf, salt, and ginger. Simmer for 20 minutes, stirring occasionally. Brush sauce over entire surface of lamb.

Place meat on grill, fat side up, over medium coals. Cook 50 minutes to an hour, basting frequently with remaining sauce and turning meat occasionally. To carve, start at one end and cut into thin slices across the grain. Makes 6 to 8 servings.

Kebab Barg
SKEWER-COOKED

A yogurt marinade gives these Iranian lamb kebabs an interesting tart flavor. It is traditionally served with a special rice dish called *chello,* which is white, fluffy, and crusty. Complete the menu with fresh vegetable relishes and Arabian flat bread or hot-buttered flour tortillas.

1 leg of lamb (5 lbs.), boned and sliced
   ½ inch thick
1 cup grated onion (or chopped and
   whirled in blender)
3 cups yogurt
1/16 teaspoon powdered saffron (optional)
   Salt
   Pepper
   About ½ cup butter
   Chello (recipe below)
10 egg yolks (shells reserved)

Trim fat off lamb. Cut in strips 2 inches wide and about 5 inches long. Mix onion with yogurt and saffron, if used. Put lamb in yogurt marinade; refrigerate, covered, for 12 to 48 hours. Thread each piece of meat on two thin skewers, running them lengthwise through long edges of the meat. Sprinkle with salt and pepper, and grill over hot coals for 3 to 4 minutes on each side.

To serve, put about 1 tablespoon butter on each hot serving plate and cover with a mound of chello (recipe follows). Place a half egg shell containing a raw egg yolk on top of each mound and slip meat off skewers; arrange one piece of meat on each side of rice. Each guest will mix the egg yolk with the rice and butter on his plate. Makes 10 servings.

Chello

2 cups long-grained rice
3 quarts water
2 tablespoons salt
¾ cup (1½ cubes) butter, melted
2 tablespoons water

Soak rice in water to cover for 8 hours or overnight; drain. In a 4-quart pan, bring the 3 quarts water and salt to a rapid boil; add the rice and cook 12 minutes. Drain and rinse with warm water. Put ¼ cup of the melted butter in a large pan that has a cover; add 2 tablespoons water. Carefully spoon the rice into bottom of the pan, shaping it to make a high cone. With the handle of a wooden spoon, make a hole from the peak of the cone to the bottom. Pour remaining ½ cup melted butter over the rice, cover, and cook for 15 minutes over medium heat. Lower heat as far as possible, put a folded cloth between the pot and its cover, and cook 5 minutes more. Makes 10 servings.

Lamb Sosaties with Fruit
SKEWER-COOKED

This method of cooking lamb kebabs, called *sosaties* (pronounced *so-*sah-*tees),* comes from South Africa, reportedly brought there by Malayan slaves in the seventeenth century. Today the sosaties, thin wooden skewers strung with small cubes of broiled marinated lamb, are popular as an entrée or snack. You might serve this peppery, sweet-sour meat with rice, a mixed green salad, crisp breadsticks, and an ice cream dessert.

1½ cups cider vinegar
  3 tablespoons apricot or pineapple jam
1½ tablespoons curry powder
1½ tablespoons salt
1½ tablespoons brown sugar, firmly packed
  ¼ teaspoon pepper
  4 small dried hot chile peppers, crushed
    (use only 1 or 2 for a milder marinade)
  2 medium-sized onions, sliced
  3 cloves garlic, crushed
  6 fresh lemon or orange leaves
    or 2 dried bay leaves
  4 pounds lean boneless lamb,
    cut in 1½-inch cubes
    About 6 cups fruit: pitted apricots, pineapple chunks, cantaloupe wedges, and spiced crabapples

In a pan, combine the vinegar, jam, curry powder, salt, brown sugar, pepper, chile peppers, onions, garlic, and lemon, orange, or bay leaves. Bring to a boil to blend the flavors; cool. Pour the marinade over the meat, cover, and refrigerate 8 to 10 hours or overnight, stirring occasionally. Just before you are ready to barbecue the meat, remove the pieces from the marinade and string on skewers. Place meat over medium-hot coals; grill, turning to brown all sides, a total of 15 to 20 minutes.

Strain the marinade, discarding the onions and leaves; bring liquid to a boil and simmer about 5 minutes to concentrate it. Baste the meat occasionally with the marinade. String the fruit on skewers and lay on top of the meat during the last 5 to 10 minutes cooking time. Baste the fruit and the meat with the marinade. The fruit will also help baste the meat and should be on the grill long enough to be thoroughly heated, but not too soft. Makes 8 to 12 servings.

Lamb Breast or Shanks
GRILL-COOKED

Either lamb breast or lamb shanks may be barbecued with rewarding success. Lamb breast may be placed directly on the grill, but lamb shanks should be precooked until tender before grilling. To precook shanks, braise them in a small amount of water in a heavy, covered pan.

  4 pounds lamb breast or 4 to 6 pounds
    precooked shanks
  1 cup orange juice
  ½ cup lemon juice
  2 tablespoons sugar
  ½ cup chopped, crushed mint leaves
    About ¼ cup salad oil

Marinate the lamb breast or precooked shanks in a mixture of the orange juice, lemon juice, and sugar. For the last 2 hours, add the mint leaves to the marinade. Oil the meat well; place on grill over slow fire and cook until thoroughly browned. While cooking, baste with a sauce made of ½ cup of the marinade mixed with ¼ cup salad oil. Heat remainder of the marinade and serve as a sauce with the meat. Makes 4 to 6 servings.

Butterflied Leg of Lamb with Mushrooms
GRILL-COOKED

Boned and laid out flat on the grill, a butterflied leg of lamb cooks quickly and evenly. Giant mushroom caps, which have been marinated with the lamb, go on the grill for the last 15 minutes.

  1 leg of lamb (5 to 6 lbs.), boned
  8 large mushrooms, each about 3 inches
    in diameter
  1 cup olive oil or salad oil
  ⅔ cup Burgundy
  ¼ teaspoon thyme
  ½ teaspoon oregano
  1 teaspoon salt
  ¼ teaspoon pepper
1½ cups finely chopped onion
  ¼ cup butter
    Salt
    Pepper

Slash into the thick portions of the lamb to make it lay as flat and evenly as possible. Carefully break stems from mushrooms and scrape a smooth hollow in the cap. Save stems and scraps. Marinate the lamb and mushroom caps for several hours in a mixture of the olive oil or salad oil, Burgundy, thyme, oregano, salt, and pepper. Finely chop mushroom stems and scraps; combine with the onion. Melt the butter; add mushroom-onion mixture and cook until tender. Season with salt and pepper to taste and set aside.

Lift meat from marinade and place, fat side down, on a grill 5 to 6 inches over medium-hot coals. Cook for about 45 minutes, turning frequently and basting with marinade.

About 15 minutes before lamb is done, drain mushroom caps and place, hollowed side down, on grill for 5 minutes. Turn onto rounded side and spoon into caps the onion-mushroom mixture; cook about 10 minutes more and baste once or twice with the lamb marinade. Thinly slice lamb across the grain and serve with mushrooms. Makes 8 servings.

Chelo Kebab
GRILL-COOKED

Chelo kebab is Persian for shish kebab. The dish includes ground lamb patties, tomatoes, and rice, so you need only a green salad and dessert to complete the menu.

1½ pounds ground lamb
1 large onion, finely chopped
1 egg
½ teaspoon salt
¼ teaspoon pepper
2 tablespoons flour
1½ cups uncooked rice
4 tablespoons butter
Paprika (optional)
3 tomatoes, halved
Butter
Salt
Pepper

Mix lamb, onion, egg, salt, pepper, and flour until smooth and creamy. Shape into oblong patties about 5 inches long, 1½ inches wide, and 1 inch thick; put aside.

Cook rice; sprinkle with cold water, shaking gently so kernels won't stick together. Drain 5 minutes. Melt butter in frying pan or shallow casserole (of a material which will stand direct heat) and pile the rice in it in a dome shape; sprinkle with paprika if desired. Place over low heat on grill or range for 10 minutes to dry rice. Meanwhile, cook lamb patties in a hinged wire broiler on barbecue for about 10 minutes on each side. Dot tomato halves with butter, salt, and pepper and place on grill for about 8 minutes. Stack cooked lamb patties on rice dome; arrange tomatoes at bottom or on separate plate. Serve hot. Makes 4 to 6 servings.

Lamb Chops a la Castellane
GRILL-COOKED

Thick-cut small loin lamb chops are served here atop grilled eggplant slices with a flavorful sauce.

3 tablespoons butter
3 tablespoons flour
1 cup rich beef stock or bouillon, undiluted
¼ cup diced lean ham
1 tablespoon butter
3 tablespoons Sherry
2 tablespoons minced green pepper
6 thick slices unpeeled eggplant
Butter or olive oil
6 loin lamb chops, cut thick
Parsley sprigs or broiled mushroom caps
for garnish

To make the sauce, melt the 3 tablespoons butter and stir in the flour. Cook, stirring, until lightly browned; then gradually add beef broth or beef bouillon. Cook until smooth and thick.

In another pan cook the ham in 1 tablespoon butter for a minute or two, then add Sherry and green pepper. Add to these ingredients thickened broth.

When the charcoal fire is good and hot, brush the eggplant on both sides with butter or olive oil, and grill until nicely browned (a hinged wire broiler makes turning easy). Keep warm on a serving platter. Broil the lamb chops so that they are pink and juicy inside, crisply brown outside. Reheat the sauce and pour over eggplant slices. Put one chop on each slice of eggplant. Garnish with sprigs of parsley or broiled mushroom caps. Makes 6 servings.

Easy Leg of Lamb
SPIT-ROASTED

A leg of lamb roasted on the spit is practically self-basting and needs little watching. It is best when still slightly pink in the center and juicy — 140° to 150° on a meat thermometer.

    1 short-cut leg of lamb (5 to 6 lbs.)
    4 cloves garlic, split
    ½ teaspoon crumbled dried oregano
    1 teaspoon salt
    4 tablespoons melted butter
      Juice of 1 lemon

Make several cuts in the leg of lamb and insert the garlic and a mixture of the oregano and salt. With any remaining oregano and salt, rub the outside of the meat. Insert the spit almost parallel to the bone and place over medium coals. Mix melted butter and the lemon juice and brush the meat. Basting once or twice, barbecue 1¼ to 1½ hours (140° to 150° on a meat thermometer) for medium rare. Makes 6 to 8 servings.

Lime-Basted Leg of Lamb
SPIT-ROASTED

Partially boned leg of lamb is easy to balance on a spit and easy to carve and serve. Order a leg of lamb with the shank bone and the aitchbone (pronounced *H-bone*) removed, and the roast tied. One long straight bone will remain near the center of the roast for balancing the meat on the rotisserie.

1 leg of lamb (about 7 lbs.), shank bone
    and aitchbone removed, tied

Guide the spit through the center of the roast parallel with the remaining bone; secure with meat prongs. Start the spit revolving over slowly burning coals or an electric unit. Baste liberally with the lime sauce (recipe follows) as the meat roasts. For best results, use a meat thermometer; cook to about 150° for juicy pink lamb. Time will be about 2 to 2½ hours. Makes about 12 servings.

Lime Basting Sauce

    1 can (6 oz.) daiquiri mix
    ½ cup dry white wine
    2 tablespoons butter or margarine
    ½ teaspoon crushed rosemary

In a small pan, combine the daiquiri mix, wine, butter or margarine, and rosemary; heat until the butter melts.

Basque-Barbecued Lamb
SPIT-ROASTED

Huge summertime picnics held by Basque communities have spread news of Basque culinary expertise. In this method for barbecuing lamb, seasoned bacon rolls are inserted in the meat to add extra flavor as it cooks. Complete the Basque menu by serving grilled Spanish chorizo sausages, baked beans, mixed green salad, marinated garbanzo beans, and warm sourdough French bread. Dessert could be an orange flan (custard) and coffee.

    ¼ cup dry Sherry
    2 tablespoons olive oil
    2 teaspoons mixed herbs (prepared herb
      blend can be used)
    1 leg of lamb (6 to 7 lbs.), boned
    2 slices bacon
      Finely chopped green onion or
      instant minced onion
      Mixed herbs for lamb
      Basting sauce (recipe follows)

Prepare a marinade of the Sherry, olive oil, and mixed herbs. Marinate the lamb overnight. Drain, saving all the marinade.

Sprinkle each slice of bacon with finely chopped green onion or instant minced onion and mixed herbs; roll up like a jelly roll; then cut each roll crosswise to make 2 smaller rolls. Cut 3 or 4 deep incisions in the thickest parts of the meat and insert a seasoned bacon roll deep into each.

Fold the boned lamb into a compact shape, tucking any ends inside. Skewer the meat together with metal or heavy wooden skewers. Then put the meat on a spit for barbecuing, or on a grill arranged about 1½ feet above the bed of glowing coals. Turn and baste often with the basting sauce (recipe follows). Barbecuing will take about 1½ hours. Makes 8 to 10 servings.

Basting Sauce

To the drained marinade (above) add: ½ cup catsup, ¼ cup wine vinegar, 1 can (6 oz.) tomato paste, 1 teaspoon liquid smoke, ½ teaspoon salt, 1 finely mashed clove garlic (or ⅛ teaspoon garlic powder), and 1 cup dry white wine. Blend the mixture well and use to baste the lamb.

Smoked Leg of Lamb
SMOKE-COOKED

You'll need to begin marinating this meat 8 hours before you plan to cook it. Truss the bone end of the lamb if you plan to cook the meat in a Chinese smoke oven; the meat hangs from this cord.

6-pound leg of lamb (bone should not be
   cracked nor end bone cut off)
2 medium-sized onions, peeled and sliced
1 tablespoon salt
½ teaspoon pepper
½ cup Sherry or orange juice
2 tablespoons olive oil
1 teaspoon oregano
½ teaspoon savory

In a pan large enough to hold the meaty portion of the
leg of lamb, combine onions, salt, pepper, Sherry or
orange juice, olive oil, oregano, and summer savory. Rub
mixture evenly over leg of lamb, and let stand at least
8 hours. Insert meat thermometer into thickest portion of
the meat, if you wish.

Build barbecue fire about an hour before you plan to
begin cooking. Hang the meat from the trussed end in
the chimney if you're using a Chinese smoke oven; or, if
you're using another covered barbecue, lay the meat on
the grill. Cook in medium heat (300° to 350°) about
2¼ hours, or until meat thermometer registers about
150°. Makes about 8 to 10 servings.

Lela ka Kabab
GRILL-COOKED

A spicy brown yogurt sauce serves as the marinade, basting sauce, and final meat sauce for these lamb steaks or
chops. As you blend it, the quantity and varied frag-
rances of the eight spices may seem a little overwhelm-
ing, but don't be alarmed; this recipe from northern India
turns out superbly seasoned.

   2 medium-sized onions, sliced
   2 tablespoons ground coriander or 6 sprigs
      fresh coriander (Chinese parsley) plus
      1 tablespoon ground coriander
   2 teaspoons salt
   2 teaspoons ground cumin
   1½ teaspoons black pepper
   1½ teaspoons ground cloves
   1½ teaspoons ground cardamom
   1 teaspoon ginger
   1 teaspoon cinnamon
   1 teaspoon poppy seeds
   2 tablespoons ghee (see explanation at end
      of recipe) or 2½ tablespoons melted butter
   1 pint (2 cups) yogurt
   6 tablespoons lemon juice
   12 lamb steaks or round bone lamb chops

Put the onions, coriander, salt, cumin, pepper, cloves,
cardamom, ginger, cinnamon, poppy seeds, ghee (see below), yogurt, and lemon juice in a blender, and blend
until smooth. (Or grind the onions and fresh coriander
with a mortar and pestle, adding spices gradually; add to

ghee, yogurt, lemon juice.) Place chops in shallow pan,
spoon over half of the marinade, and let meat marinate,
refrigerated, overnight; or let stand at room temperature
2 hours. Barbecue over glowing coals for about 40 minutes, or to desired doneness. Baste occasionally with the
sauce. You can heat the leftover marinade and serve it as
a sauce over the meat. Makes 12 servings.

(Ghee, or purified fresh butter, is made by heating 1
pound butter in a 2 or 3-quart saucepan over very low
heat for 1 hour, or until only butter fat remains. Strain
through a cheesecloth. The flavor of ghee is quite different from that of butter, and it has a higher smoking point.)

Garlic Leg of Lamb
with Coffee Baste
SMOKE-COOKED

Strong hot coffee, lots of garlic, and a two-hour smoking
give this roast its special flavor.

   5 cloves garlic, peeled
   1 leg of lamb (5 to 6 lbs.)
      Salt
      Pepper
   ⅓ cup strong hot coffee
   ⅓ cup melted butter
   1 teaspoon grated lemon peel

Insert garlic cloves in the leg of lamb; rub with salt and
pepper. Place over indirect charcoal heat (meat-level
temperature about 300°). Cover and roast with smoke
about 2 hours or until meat thermometer registers about
150°. Baste during last half of roasting time with a mixture of the coffee, melted butter, and grated lemon peel.
Slice and serve while hot. Makes 8 to 10 servings.

PORK

A smoky flavor is a natural addition to pork. To accent the richness of barbecued pork, add fruit or spice flavors with a marinade or baste.

A barbecue with a hood is needed for cooking large cuts of pork such as a leg or boned shoulder roast. Recent testing has shown that bone-in pork loin roasts and boneless leg and shoulder roasts can be safely roasted to an internal temperature of only 170°; they were found to be juicy and flavorful.

When barbecuing pork chops or steaks, choose thick cuts—preferably 1 to 1½ inches thick. Cook them slowly over moderate heat until browned, but still moist and juicy.

Spareribs, a barbecue favorite, can be barbecued by several methods. Brown them first over hot coals, then simmer in a flavorful sauce. Or, partially cook ribs in water and finish them on the barbecue.

Venezuelan Barbecued Pork
GRILL-COOKED

A surprisingly compact rectangular steak, about 1½ inches thick, results when you buy a fresh pork butt and ask your meatman to remove the bone and butterfly it. The chopped vegetable marinade is typical of Venezuelan barbecuing.

- 1 large onion, chopped
- 1 can (4 oz.) pimiento, drained and chopped
- 2 cloves garlic, minced or mashed
- ⅓ cup chopped parsley
- ½ cup white vinegar
- ¼ cup salad oil
- 1½ teaspoons salt
- ¼ teaspoon pepper
- 1 fresh pork butt (about 6 lbs.), boned and butterflied

To make the marinade, combine in a bowl the onion, pimiento, garlic, parsley, vinegar, salad oil, salt, and pepper. Set aside.

Place meat, fat side down, on working surface. With a sharp knife, score top of meat with about three lengthwise and five crosswise cuts, each about ½ inch deep. Put meat in baking dish and pour the marinade over it. Let stand 2 hours.

Scrape marinade off meat and reserve. Place meat, scored side down, over low coals. Barbecue slowly (with or without a hood on the barbecue) for 1 hour. Turn meat over and continue cooking slowly for 1 to 1½

hours, or until the meat is cooked through. (You can insert a meat thermometer into the center after the meat is turned; recommended internal temperature for this cut of pork is 170°.) Baste meat several times with the marinade after turning.

To serve, cut through score lines into individual portions. Heat remaining marinade and serve as a sauce. Makes 12 to 15 servings.

Pork Satés Bali
SKEWER-COOKED

A Far Eastern spiciness permeates pork kebabs when you use puréed chutney in the marinade. Twirl the grilled kebabs in finely chopped peanuts to lend an authentic Indonesian flavor.

Direct your meatman to bone a pork loin and slice it ¾ inch thick and then into 1-inch squares. This cut will grill quickly to a tender state.

- ½ cup chutney
- ¼ cup catsup
- 1 tablespoon soy sauce
- 4 drops liquid hot-pepper seasoning
- 2 tablespoons salad oil
- 2 pounds boneless pork loin, cut ¾ inch thick in 1-inch squares
- ¾ cup salted peanuts, very finely chopped

Purée the chutney in a blender until smooth (or finely chop it). Turn into a bowl and add catsup, soy sauce, hot-pepper seasoning, and oil. Add meat squares and let marinate for several hours, turning occasionally. Impale meat on 6 skewers. Barbecue over medium coals about 15 minutes, turning to brown all sides. Immediately roll in finely chopped peanuts, spread out on a small tray or plate, to coat all sides. Makes 6 servings.

Ham Steak with Cantaloupe
GRILL-COOKED

Total cooking time is short for this ham and fruit entrée. The precooked ham steak takes less than 20 minutes to heat through and brown on the surface; the cantaloupe takes about half that time to become hot and glazed. Hot buttered rice and a tossed green salad are ideal accompaniments.

4 tablespoons melted butter
¼ to ½ teaspoon curry powder
1 tablespoon syrup drained from chutney
1 center slice (about 1¾ lbs), precooked
   ham steak, 1 inch thick
1 medium-sized cantaloupe,
   peeled and seeded
   Chutney

Blend the butter with curry powder and syrup drained from chutney; brush on both sides of the ham steak. Place steak on grill 5 to 6 inches above medium-hot coals. Cook for 16 to 20 minutes, turning occasionally and basting frequently with the seasoned butter.

Cut cantaloupe into 6 to 8 wedges; brush with the prepared butter. About 10 minutes before ham is done, place melon on grill. Let each wedge heat for about 3 minutes on each side and the back. Serve ham and cantaloupe with chutney. Makes 5 to 6 servings.

Smoky Ham Steaks
GRILL-COOKED

Smoke from the barbecue fire and a catsup marinade add flavor to this canned ham supper entrée. To complete the meal you might serve buttered green beans, sliced tomatoes and cucumbers sprinkled with French dressing, buttered bread heated on the barbecue, and ice cream or sherbet.

Combine ½ cup catsup, ½ cup water, and ½ cup salad oil with 4 small crushed cloves garlic. Cut a 3-pound fully cooked canned ham into approximately 8 slices, each about ¾ inch thick. Pour part of the marinade into a large shallow pan, arrange slices in pan, and pour remaining marinade over them; cover and refrigerate several hours, turning slices occasionally in the marinade. Barbecue ham slices about 3 minutes on each side or until hot and lightly browned. Strain marinade and discard garlic; heat and serve with the ham. Makes about 8 servings.

Rolled Leg of Pork, Hawaiian-Style
SPIT-ROASTED

A rolled leg of fresh pork looks impressive coming off the barbecue spit. It compares to that dramatic moment at a luau when the pit is uncovered and the whole cooked pig is removed.

Order a whole leg of fresh pork (about 12 pounds) and have the meatman bone and roll it. Prepare the pork marinade (recipe follows) and marinate the pork for at least 1 hour. Place meat on spit, and roast over medium coals until well done, about 6 hours for a 12-pound roast (internal temperature on meat thermometer should read 170°). Baste frequently with the marinade as meat roasts. When done, remove from spit, slice and serve on a large platter. Add 1 cup applesauce (left from making the marinade) to the remaining marinade; heat and serve with the sliced meat. Makes 12 servings.

Apple-Soy Marinade for Pork

Combine half of a 1-pound can of applesauce (about 1 cup) with ¾ cup dry white wine, ½ cup soy sauce, 2 tablespoons salad oil, 1 cup chopped onion, 1 clove garlic, minced or mashed, and 1 teaspoon ground ginger; mix well.

Spicy Ham Steak
GRILL-COOKED

Barbecue this ham steak at home or carry it to a picnic in its marinade. You might accompany it with a hot or cold vegetable soup, sweet potato salad, cherry tomatoes, fruit tarts, and beverage.

¼ cup melted butter
1 cup Sherry
1 cup pineapple juice
2 teaspoons ground cloves
¼ cup dry mustard
¼ cup firmly packed brown sugar
2 teaspoons paprika
1½ cloves garlic, minced
1 center-cut slice ham, 1 inch thick

Combine the melted butter, Sherry, pineapple juice, cloves, mustard, brown sugar, paprika, and garlic. Slash edges of ham and marinate in this mixture for 3 hours, turning several times. Grill over low to medium coals for 20 minutes, basting frequently with marinade and turning occasionally. Carve ham into individual portions and serve hot. Makes about 4 servings.

Crumb-Coated Pigs' Feet
GRILL-COOKED

The pigs' feet must be boiled before they are grilled. Cook them, whole or split, in water to cover, with salt, an onion, and an herb bouquet. Simmer until tender— from 3 to 4 hours. Drain, brush well with softened butter, then roll in fine dry bread or cracker crumbs. Grill until nicely browned on all sides. Serve with charcoal-roasted potatoes and sauerkraut heated in a pot at the back of the grill.

Ginger-Barbecued Spareribs
GRILL-COOKED

Slivers of candied ginger are sprinkled onto the red glaze of the barbecue sauce at serving time. Try salted pine nuts as a side dish.

1 can (8 oz.) tomato sauce
1 can (about 1 lb.) tomato purée
¼ cup wine vinegar
¼ cup brown sugar
1 tablespoon Worcestershire
1 lemon slice
1 medium-sized onion, finely chopped, or
1 tablespoon dried minced onions
1 clove garlic, crushed
1 teaspoon salt
½ teaspoon chile powder
½ teaspoon celery salt
½ teaspoon dry mustard
⅛ teaspoon pepper
About 6 pounds country-style spareribs
2 tablespoons finely chopped or
slivered candied ginger

Make this barbecue sauce: Combine in a saucepan the tomato sauce, tomato purée, wine vinegar, brown sugar, Worcestershire, lemon, onion, garlic, salt, chile powder, celery salt, dry mustard, and pepper. Cover and simmer 20 minutes, stirring occasionally.

Barbecue spareribs over low coals for about 1½ hours. Turn frequently, basting with sauce. When ready to serve, sprinkle spareribs with ginger. Makes 8 servings.

Pork Loin with Prunes
SMOKE-COOKED

A prune-stuffed rack of pork can be smoked even when the weather is brisk, for it requires little tending. It acquires a rich smoke flavor and deep brown color in about 2 hours.

Buy a loin of pork that weighs about 6½ to 7½ pounds. Have your meatman cut through the meaty portion, making cuts about 2 inches apart to the bone (you will stuff these cuts with prunes before roasting the meat). Have the loin bones cracked to make serving easier.

Soak ½ pound large pitted prunes in 1 cup Sherry, port, or orange juice for 2 hours. Stuff prunes into cuts in the pork loin—2 or 3 prunes in each pocket. Tie the whole loin lengthwise to keep the pockets from opening while cooking. Insert a meat thermometer into the center of the meat. Place meat on the grill, cook over an even bed of coals in medium heat (300° to 350°) about 2 hours, or until thermometer registers 170°. Baste meat occasionally with liquid in which prunes were soaked. Makes 6 servings.

Spit-Roasted Suckling Pig

SPIT-ROASTED

It is the ambition of every barbecue chef to try his hand at a roast suckling pig. If you have decided that the time has come for you to undertake this cooking venture, ask your meatman to provide you with a cleaned, tender suckling pig about 15 to 20 pounds in weight. A young pig any smaller would be nothing but skin and bones when cooked.

Stuff the pig with a sage or fruit dressing. Don't stuff too tightly, as the dressing will expand. Sew it in with heavy string and lace it closely and tightly.

Leave the skin on. Head and feet can be cut off either before or after cooking; it is more easily done before, but it won't look much like a pig. Insert a piece of wood in the mouth to simplify adding an apple later. Truss the legs with cord in a kneeling position and place the pig on a spit over a deep bed of hot coals.

The coals should be arranged in such a way to allow for a pan to be placed in the center to catch drippings from the roasting meat; drippings should be used for basting. The pig can be basted with oil, but it will lose some of its flavor. Allow about 6 to 10 hours cooking time.

When done, remove pig from the spit; place a red apple in the mouth and cranberries or cherries in the eye sockets; then place pig on a bed of watercress. Various garnishes of vegetable flowers, radish roses, stuffed stewed apricots and prunes, or holly berries may be added.

Bring the roast pig to the table with the head separated from the body and the cut ringed with a wreath of watercress and flowers. In carving, first separate the shoulder from the carcass and remove the legs. This will leave the ribs open to the knife. Cut down the backbone; remove the loins and serve the tender chops from the sliced loins.

Hickory-Smoked Ham
for a Crowd

SMOKE-COOKED

A whole ham is rubbed with a mustard-clove mixture and basted with Sherry as it cooks. Hickory chips are added to the fire during the last hour of cooking to give the ham a hickory-smoked flavor.

Buy a precooked ham, about 16 pounds. Score with a sharp knife, rub with a mixture of 3 tablespoons prepared mustard and 2 teaspoons ground cloves. Build barbecue fire about an hour before you start cooking. Arrange ham over foil drip pan (you can make a foil pan or use an old metal cake pan, about 9 by 12 inches). Insert a meat thermometer into the thickest portion of the ham.

Cover barbecue with its lid or a blanket of foil and cook over medium heat (300° to 350° grill temperature) until the meat thermometer reaches 145°; it takes about 3½ hours. Baste while cooking with 1 cup Sherry or orange juice. Before last hour of cooking, sprinkle fire with a handful of damp hickory chips. Makes approximately 20 generous servings.

Pineapple Spareribs

GRILL-COOKED

Pineapple is the special touch in these spareribs, proportioned to serve a holiday crowd of 10 to 12 people. You can precook these ribs at home and finish them on the barbecue at your picnic site. Brush with Pineapple Baste or another favorite barbecue sauce.

```
10 pounds spareribs
   Water
12 whole black peppers
 6 whole cloves
 2 bay leaves
 2 cloves garlic
   Sweet-Sour Pineapple Baste
   (recipe on page 82)
```

Place spareribs in water that almost covers; season with black peppers, cloves, bay leaves, and garlic. (If you don't have a pan large enough, cook half the ribs at a time, using half the seasonings each time.) Simmer for 30 minutes, or until almost tender. Drain, then refrigerate, covered.

To finish cooking, arrange spareribs on the barbecue grill over hot coals; cook about 30 minutes turning occasionally. During the last 15 minutes of cooking, baste with your favorite barbecue sauce. Cook until ribs are glazed and tender. Remove ribs to warm platter. Makes 10 to 12 servings.

Garlic Spareribs
SPIT-ROASTED

Those who favor garlic will approve these spit-roasted spareribs.

    About 6 pounds spareribs
  4 large cloves garlic
  1 tablespoon salt
  1 cup chicken broth
  1 cup orange marmalade
  ¼ cup vinegar
  ¼ cup catsup

Figure on at least 1 pound of spareribs per person. Leave the side whole so you can thread them on a spit later. Combine the garlic, salt, chicken broth, marmalade, vinegar, and catsup. Marinate the spareribs for at least 12 hours in this mixture, turning several times. Weave the whole strips on a spit, and cook over low coals for 1 to 1½ hours, or until shiny brown and fork tender. Baste with the marinade during the cooking. Makes 6 servings.

Smoked Ribs in Barbecue Sauce
SMOKE-COOKED

A covered barbecue is recommended for cooking these thick, meaty country-style spareribs. Use part of the sauce to baste the meat, then put the cooked meat into the sauce to simmer for 20 to 30 minutes.

  1 cup catsup
  1 cup water
  1 cup dry white wine or Sherry
  ¼ cup Worcestershire
  1 medium-sized onion, sliced
  1 whole lemon; thinly sliced
  1 clove garlic, sliced
  2 tablespoons butter or margarine
  4 pounds country-style spareribs
    Salt
    Pepper

To make the barbecue sauce, combine in a pan (one that's large enough to hold the spareribs) the catsup, water, wine, Worcestershire, onion, lemon, garlic, and butter or margarine. Bring to boiling, reduce heat, cover, and simmer slowly for 30 minutes. This much can be done ahead.

To grill the meat, first sprinkle both sides of spareribs lightly with salt and pepper. Place, fat side up, on the grill over slowly burning coals. Put lid on barbecue and adjust drafts, if any, to keep fire burning slowly.

Cook about 1 hour to 1 hour and 20 minutes, turning several times and basting often with part of the barbecue sauce (put about 1 cup of the sauce into a small pan to use for basting). Reheat the rest of the barbecue sauce in the pan; as the rib pieces are cooked, remove from grill, cut into individual servings, and put into the sauce. Cover pan and simmer 20 to 30 minutes. Spoon some of the sauce over each piece as you serve it. Makes about 6 servings.

Barbecued Bacon with Pineapple
GRILL-COOKED

Serve this breakfast entrée with scrambled eggs and your favorite muffins. Watch the bacon carefully, turning frequently, and be sure the coals are low; you want to brown the meat slowly for a nice crisp texture, without flare-ups from the drippings.

8 slices bacon cut from a slab,
  each cut ½ inch thick
4 slices fresh pineapple, each about ½ inch
  thick, peeled (or substitute drained
  canned pineapple slices)
  Melted butter or margarine

Arrange bacon on grill about 4 inches above slow coals. Cook about 25 minutes, turning frequently, or until the bacon is crisp and richly browned.

About 15 minutes before bacon is ready, also place on grill the pineapple slices brushed with melted butter or margarine. Cook about 5 minutes on each side or until hot and lightly browned, turning with a spatula. Makes 4 servings.

Chinese Ribs
SMOKE-COOKED

The trick of drying the honey-marinated meat before cooking plays about the most important part in the resulting crispy surface texture of these spareribs.

    About 6 pounds spareribs
¼ cup soy sauce
 1 teaspoon pepper
 4 tablespoons honey
¼ cup Sherry

Marinate whole sides of the spareribs in a mixture of the soy sauce, pepper, honey, and Sherry for at least 30 minutes. Remove the ribs from the marinade and allow to dry thoroughly.

Hang the ribs from the top of a moderate (300° to 400°) Chinese smoke oven for 1¼ to 1½ hours. The closer you place the ribs to the actual fire, the more carefully you have to watch for charring. Makes 6 servings.

Honey-Glazed Ham
SMOKE-COOKED

You'll need a covered smoke cooker, or a barbecue with a cover that encloses the grill for this ham. (See page 14 for directions on making a foil cover.)

Place a drip-catching pan in center of grill beneath ham. If you don't have a suitable ready-made pan, you can make one of heavy-duty foil folded double. Make it about 3 inches longer and 2 inches wider than the ham, with sides about 2½ inches high.

Start two charcoal piles (one on each side of the drip pan) of 20 briquets each, 30 to 45 minutes before you plan to start the ham (the briquets should burn down to an even gray). After each hour of cooking time, add about 6 briquets on each side.

Start the ham on the grill 3 to 5 hours before serving time, depending on the size and type of ham you buy. Plan on 15 to 20 minutes per pound if you buy a "tenderized" ham (or cook to 160° on meat thermometer); 10 to 15 minutes per pound for a fully cooked ham (or 130° on meat thermometer).

As an added precaution to keep ham fat away from the barbecue fire, shape a "pan" of double heavy-duty foil loosely around lower half of ham. Sides should be about 4 inches high and should stand away from ham about 1 inch all around. This pan will catch most of the ham drippings—and the drip pan below will catch the rest. Insert the meat thermometer in thick portion of ham.

Set ham on the barbecue, centered over drip pan. For slow heat, keep any draft opening small. Check the ham every half hour; if it begins to brown too quickly,

lower heat by making draft openings smaller (but don't completely close them). If drippings accumulate excessively in the pan directly under the ham, remove them with a meat baster. One hour before ham is done, remove from barbecue, drain off drippings, skin, score, and brush with honey glaze (recipe follows). Return to barbecue and brush with glaze about every 15 minutes. When ham is done, it will be easier to slice if you let it stand 15 to 20 minutes.

Honey Glaze

Combine 3 tablespoons honey, 1 tablespoon Worcestershire, 1 tablespoon dry mustard, ¾ teaspoon ground ginger, and a dash of black pepper; mix well.

Roast Pork Loin on Melon Ring
SMOKE-COOKED

Here's a mouthwatering combination: Thick slices of smoked pork atop smoked cantaloupe rings with whipped cream cheese and chives over all.

Place a 4-pound rolled pork loin roast over moderate coals (grill thermometer should read about 300°). Cover and roast for 2 hours or until meat thermometer registers 170°. Peel cantaloupe; cut one ½-inch thick ring for each serving. Brush with butter and place on sheet of foil; put on grill to heat and smoke for 10 minutes (while you slice pork roast). Have ready 2 small packages (3 oz. *each*) cream cheese with chives, beaten with ½ cup heavy cream until fluffy. To serve, place a thick pork slice atop a melon ring. Top with a spoonful of whipped cheese. Makes about 12 servings.

VARIETY MEATS

People tend to forget variety meats when they decide to barbecue. However, you will find the combination of the barbecue smoke flavor and a marinade or baste on liver, tongue, and the other variety meats surprisingly different. One of the following recipes may even become a family favorite!

Foie de Veau en Brochette
SKEWER-COOKED

Serve these French-style calf liver squares plain, or with Sauce Bercy for Grilled Meats.

    Sauce Bercy for Grilled Meats
    (see page 81)
 2 pounds calf liver, sliced ½ inch thick,
    then cut in 1-inch squares
 ½ cup (¼ lb.) hot melted butter
 ½ pound sliced bacon, cut in squares
    Fine dry bread crumbs

Stiffen liver by dipping it in the hot melted butter. Cook bacon in the butter for 2 or 3 minutes. Thread the liver on skewers, alternating with the bacon. Dip in the melted butter, roll in fine dry bread crumbs, then grill over hot coals until lightly browned. Makes 6 servings.

Brochette de Rognons d'Agneau
SKEWER-COOKED

12 lamb kidneys
   Melted butter
   Sauce Bercy for Grilled Meats
   (see page 81)

Remove the fat and skin from the kidneys; split from the inside edge to within ½ inch of the opposite side. Open up and remove the white membrane from inside each kidney. Thread on skewers, using a big stitch to hold kidneys open. Brush with melted butter and grill over hot coals, basting with butter, for 3 to 4 minutes on each side. Be careful not to overcook them or they will be tough. Serve with Sauce Bercy for Grilled Meats (see page 81). Makes 4 to 6 servings.

Mi'Laaf Mashivi
SKEWER-COOKED

This liver recipe from Lebanon is so simple that it might well become a family standby. Serve it with lemon wedges and hot rice.

 1 clove garlic, puréed
 ¼ cup olive oil
 2 teaspoons salt
 ¼ cup chopped fresh mint
 1 tablespoon lemon juice
 ⅛ teaspoon freshly ground black pepper
 2 pounds beef liver, sliced ½ inch thick
 3 to 4 tablespoons olive oil

Mix together garlic, the ¼ cup olive oil, salt, mint, lemon juice, and pepper. Spread this mixture on both sides of the liver and let stand for 2 hours. Cut into 2-inch squares. Thread liver on two skewers, keeping meat flat. Grill quickly over hot coals, 1½ to 2 minutes on each side, basting with the remaining marinade mixed with the 3 to 4 tablespoons olive oil. The meat should be pink and juicy inside. Makes about 6 servings.

Tripe Strips in Butter
GRILL-COOKED

You might serve fried onions and green pepper, and roasted potatoes with this tripe for supper.

Like tongue, tripe needs pre-cooking until fork-tender. Do it in a pressure cooker or by boiling in salted water. Cut in strips, dip in melted butter, and grill on both sides until brown. Serve with individual dishes of melted butter and wedges of lemon.

Barbecued Kidneys
GRILL-COOKED

Beef, veal, lamb, and pork kidneys may all be successfully cooked over charcoal. Split the kidneys and remove cores; brush with oil or melted butter, seasoned, if you wish, with garlic or with bacon drippings. Grill over a medium hot fire 5 to 15 minutes, depending on size. They are done when brown on the outside but still pink and juicy inside; don't overcook. Slice and serve with melted butter.

Kidneys may also be cut in pieces, wrapped in bacon, and then charcoal-broiled. In this case it is not necessary to brush them with oil. Cook until bacon is very crisp. Serve with broiled tomatoes or, if desired, as part of a mixed grill with broiled sausage and lamb chops or liver.

Peruvian Anticuchos
SKEWER-COOKED

Beef heart cubes marinated in this spicy sauce and cooked to perfection are tender and flavorful. If you wish, skewer meat alternately with mushroom caps.

    1 beef heart (about 3 lbs.)
1½ teaspoons salt
1½ teaspoons chile powder
 ½ teaspoon freshly ground pepper
    2 cloves garlic, puréed
 ½ cup vinegar
 ¼ cup water
 ½ cup olive oil

Trim beef heart of all hard fat; remove the tubes. Cut into 1-inch cubes. Marinate overnight in a mixture of salt, chile powder, pepper, garlic, vinegar, water, and olive oil. String cubes well apart on thin skewers. Grill over hot coals about 3 minutes on all four sides (12 minutes in all), basting 3 or 4 times with the marinade. Don't overcook. Makes 6 servings.

Liver 'n Bacon Grill
SKEWER-COOKED

Bacon drippings that fall on the coals and make the fire flare up give the liver a wonderful barbecue smoke flavor. Ask your meatman for thick-sliced liver to make these liver and bacon rolls.

2 pounds calf liver (about 4 pieces,
    cut 1 inch thick)
8 strips lean bacon

Have the meatman cut liver into 1-inch-thick slices and trim off veins and outer skin. Soak liver in a mild salt-water solution (1 teaspoon salt to 2 cups water) for 30 minutes. Remove from water and dry surfaces of liver. Put a strip of bacon under each piece and another on top of it; then roll up and secure with a skewer.

Place liver in marinade (recipe follows) and marinate in the refrigerator for 2 or 3 hours, turning twice during that time.

Put liver on grill over medium charcoal fire. Grill on each side, turning only once (approximately 15 minutes total cooking time). *Do not overcook.* The meat should be slightly pink on the inside with a mild brown crust on the outside. Makes 4 to 6 servings.

Marinade

½ cup olive or salad oil
⅛ teaspoon pepper
⅛ teaspoon garlic salt or
    ¼ teaspoon onion salt

Combine salad oil, pepper, and salt.

Liver Superb
GRILL-COOKED

Liver is at its best when cooked over charcoal. Serve it with bacon and fried onions, broiled tomatoes, or eggplant.

Use beef, veal, or lamb liver, and have it sliced at least 1 inch thick. Brush well with melted butter, oil, or bacon drippings. Grill over a medium-hot fire, allowing the meat to become crisply brown on the outside, pink and juicy but not dry in the middle. (Most people prefer liver grilled medium-rare.) Make a slit in the meat with a sharp knife to test degree of doneness.

Marinated Liver Steak
GRILL-COOKED

If you always cook liver sliced, this recipe may surprise you, for the liver is the size and shape of a thick steak.

1½ cups dry red wine
¾ cup chicken stock
2 tablespoons olive oil
1 tablespoon vinegar
1 tablespoon lemon juice
½ medium-sized onion, chopped
½ cup minced parsley
1½ bay leaves, crushed
1 teaspoon whole thyme
½ teaspoon whole basil
¼ teaspoon whole oregano
¼ teaspoon whole tarragon
¼ teaspoon whole rosemary
2-pound piece beef liver, 2 to 2½ inches thick

Combine in a pan the wine, chicken stock, oil, vinegar, lemon juice, onion, parsley, bay leaves, thyme, basil, oregano, tarragon, and rosemary. Bring to a boil, reduce heat, and simmer 2 minutes. Cook 5 to 10 minutes; then pour over liver. Cover and refrigerate for 24 hours to 3 days.

To cook liver, drain and place over medium-hot coals, 10 to 12 minutes per side (for rare); turn once and baste often with marinade. (To see if done, make a small cut in center of meat.) To serve, carve crosswise slices, ¼ inch thick. Makes about 6 servings.

Butter-Broiled Brains
GRILL-COOKED

Beef, veal, or lamb brains may be grilled over charcoal. Since they vary in size, here's a serving guide: a beef brain serves three, a veal brain serves two, and a lamb brain serves one. Unless you are a master of fire control and charcoal cookery, it is best to parboil the brains first.

Soak brains in cold water, then simmer for 15 minutes in water to cover. (Add 1 tablespoon lemon juice and 1 teaspoon salt to each quart of water.) Drain, and cover with ice water; remove discolored spots. Drain again. Split

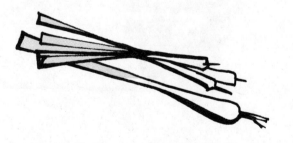

brains and dip in melted butter, then roll in fine dry bread or cracker crumbs.

Grill over a low charcoal fire, turning so that both sides will brown. Cook about 10 minutes, basting occasionally with a little more butter. Serve them with lemon wedges, crisp bacon, and drawn butter or tartare sauce.

Individual Meat and Spinach Loaves
GRILL-COOKED

Ground pork, beef, and chopped spinach are the principle ingredients in these small meat loaves.

Crumble ½ pound ground lean pork into a frying pan; add ½ medium-sized onion, finely chopped, and sauté until pork loses its pink color and onion is soft. Crush 15 round butter crackers to make ½ cup fine crumbs. Beat 1 egg slightly; blend in cracker crumbs. Add pork mixture, 1 pound ground beef chuck, 1 cup chopped fresh spinach (or ½ cup well drained, thawed, frozen spinach), ¼ cup dry red wine (optional), and a dash pepper. Mix gently to blend, using your hands if you wish. Shape mixture into 6 oval loaves about 2 inches thick.

Place on grill over slowly burning coals and barbecue about 45 minutes, turning carefully several times and brushing frequently with tomato-soy sauce (recipe below), until loaves are well browned. Makes 6 servings.

Tomato-Soy Sauce

Blend ½ cup canned tomato sauce, ¼ cup dry red wine, 2 tablespoons soy sauce, 1 tablespoon salad oil, and 1 bay leaf in small pan. Warm at edge of grill while loaves cook.

Barbecued Sausages
GRILL-COOKED

A trip to your local supermarket or delicatessen can yield an assortment of interesting sausages, which make fine eating for a picnic or supper. Here are suggestions for sausages you might try and the cooking that each type requires:

Swiss sausage (bratwurst) — Cover with cold water, bring slowly to just under the simmering point (the water must never boil or the sausage will burst), cover pan, remove from heat, and let stand for 10 minutes. Heat slowly on the grill just until lightly browned and hot.

Italian simmering sausage (coteghino) — Cook in simmering water to cover for 45 minutes. Reheat and brown on grill.

Blood sausage (French boudin or Italian biroldo Toscano) — Heat through slowly on the grill.

Cocktail sausages — String on skewers to heat on grill.

Frankfurters, exposition frankfurters — These need no precooking; just grill slowly until heated through.

German garlic sausage (knackwurst) — Cook slowly on the grill just until brown and heated through.

Italian garlic sausage (salsiccia) — Simmer gently in water to cover for 30 minutes. Grill slowly until heated and browned.

Smoked Polish sausage (kielbasa or kolbassy) — Barbecue slowly until browned and heated through.

Thick-Sliced Beef Heart
GRILL-COOKED

If you like rare beef, you will like beef heart sliced ½ inch thick and grilled quickly over charcoal. The slices should first be marinated in equal parts wine and olive oil, or in melted butter. If cooked lightly, the heart will be tender. Do not attempt this method if you like your beef well done, for longer grilling will make the beef heart tough.

Hickory-Smoked Tongue
SMOKE-COOKED

Smoked beef tongue is delicious hot or cold. Here it can be served in sandwiches or as hors d'oeuvres.

Cook a medium-sized beef tongue in simmering water until tender; skin and trim. Place on grill, cover, and smoke-cook with hickory smoke over very low indirect heat for 2 hours. After an hour's smoking, baste occasionally with mixture of 2 tablespoons tomato purée, 2 tablespoons melted butter, ¼ teaspoon crumbled whole basil, and ⅛ teaspoon crumbled whole tarragon. Slice thinly and serve either hot or cold for sandwiches. Serve cold for hors d'oeuvres.

Broiled Tongue
SPIT-ROASTED

Tongue needs precooking, but it is very good barbecued until crusty outside.

  1 beef tongue
½ cup melted butter
½ cup dry white wine
  1 teaspoon chopped chives
  1 teaspoon chopped parsley
  1 teaspoon whole tarragon

Cook tongue in a pressure cooker or in boiling water until tender. Drain, skin, and trim. Put tongue on a spit and cook over charcoal for about 45 minutes, basting with a mixture of the melted butter, wine, chives, parsley, and tarragon.

Whole Liver with Salt Pork
SPIT-ROASTED

Serve this delicious meat, sliced fairly thin, with parsley-buttered new potatoes and foil-wrapped onions roasted in the coals. Corn on the cob is also a good accompaniment.

Select a whole calf or lamb liver and tie it into a compact piece. Lard it or tie strips of salt pork on the outside. Insert spit and cook liver over a medium-hot fire for about an hour, or until a meat thermometer reads 150° for juicy pink, 160° for well done.

Barbecued Bologna
GRILL-COOKED

Barbecued bologna with a special baste makes a hit with teenagers. Try it for an outdoor late breakfast with fresh fruit and warm coffee cake.

Buy a 3-pound roll of bologna and cut it in half lengthwise. Remove casing from the bologna. Score the entire surface making cuts 1 inch apart and ¼ inch deep and stud it with 24 whole cloves. Skewer both halves or set them on a piece of foil (if cooking on a covered barbecue), and grill over hot coals or on a rotisserie. Turn and baste bologna with a mixture of ½ cup red currant jelly and 2 tablespoons prepared hot mustard.

If you cook the meat in a covered barbecue, turn it once to baste both top and bottom evenly, and cook with barbecue cover on. Cook for 30 to 45 minutes or until well glazed and hot. Makes 10 to 12 servings. (Leftovers make excellent sandwiches.)

GAME

In order to enjoy wild game, a hunter must first have a successful hunting trip. Then, in the flush of his success, he can turn chef and barbecue the roasts, steaks, and chops for a special occasion.

Today it's also possible to do big-game hunting right in the supermarket. Occasionally you may find a store selling buffalo meat—generally a brief, special sale in the fall. Buffalo cuts are similar to beef in tenderness and can be cooked in much the same way.

Recipes in this section are for those special occasions when you might have venison or buffalo suitable for barbecuing. These meats are less marbled with fat than is beef; if young, tender, and properly aged, it doesn't need marinating. However, a marinade is recommended for older animals, and it adds flavor to any cut. When barbecued, game meat requires quick cooking and frequent basting with melted butter or a seasoned butter baste.

Buffalo in Tomato-Wine Sauce
GRILL-COOKED

Here is a way to use boneless buffalo stew meat. Searing the meat first over a barbecue fire gives it a pleasantly smoky flavor that enhances the tomato sauce. If you cook this stew entirely on the barbecue, use a heavy cast iron pan.

2½ pounds buffalo stew meat
 1 large onion, thinly sliced and
    separated into rings
 ⅓ cup olive oil or salad oil
 1 cup Burgundy
 1 cup regular strength beef broth
 1 cup tomato purée
 1 bay leaf
 1 teaspoon salt
 ⅛ teaspoon pepper
    Buttered noodles

Sear buffalo meat on oiled barbecue grill over glowing coals, turning to brown on all sides. Remove, cool slightly, and cut into 1-inch cubes (if necessary). In pan, sauté onion in heated oil until soft; add meat. Blend in wine; cook quickly until wine is reduced by half. Stir in broth, tomato purée, bay leaf, salt, and pepper. Cover and simmer slowly (over the charcoal or on your range) for about 1 hour, or until meat is very tender. Remove bay leaf. Serve over noodles. Makes 4 to 6 servings.

Grilled Venison Steak
GRILL-COOKED

Have steaks cut thick—never less than 1 inch, preferably 1½ inches. Rub with garlic, if you wish; brush with olive oil or butter, and grill over hot coals 8 to 14 minutes, depending on the thickness of the steak and rareness desired. Connoisseurs prefer venison rare.

Venison Steak with Trio of Butters
GRILL-COOKED

Trim fat from good quality venison steaks or chops; brush with oil. Grill over charcoal until rare or medium-rare. Remove to hot platter; sprinkle lightly with seasoned salt and coarse black pepper. Serve with a selection of three seasoned butters, to be spooned onto steak.

Green Chile Butter

To make this seasoned butter, simply blend 1 tablespoon finely chopped canned green chile into ½ cup softened butter.

Sesame-Cheese Butter

Scatter 1 teaspoon sesame seeds on baking sheet; lightly brown in 400° oven. Blend toasted sesame seeds and 2 tablespoons crumbled Roquefort or shredded Cheddar cheese into ½ cup softened butter.

Vegetable Butter

Blend 2 tablespoons chopped onion and ¼ cup peeled and finely grated carrot into ½ cup softened butter.

Venison Roast with Cinnamon Apples
SPIT-ROASTED

This venison roast, to be cooked on your barbecue rotisserie, should be of even diameter and tied, if necessary. It's basted with a spicy barbecue sauce. You can prepare the cinnamon apple garnish while the meat roasts.

  1 venison roast (about 5 lbs.), fat trimmed off
¼ pound salt pork
  2 or 3 cloves garlic
½ cup sage honey
⅔ cup soy sauce
  1 cup orange juice
⅔ cup catsup
  1 cup wine vinegar
  1 teaspoon salt
  1 teaspoon dry mustard
  1 teaspoon paprika
½ teaspoon liquid hot-pepper seasoning
    Cinnamon apples (recipe follows)
    Spiced peaches (optional)

Wipe roast with a damp cloth or paper towel. Slice salt pork into thin strips, peel and sliver garlic cloves. Make slits in the roast and insert the salt pork and garlic slivers.

To make basting sauce, combine in a small pan the honey, soy sauce, orange juice, catsup, vinegar, salt, mustard, paprika, and liquid hot-pepper seasoning.

Insert a meat thermometer in the thickest part of the meat, but without touching the bone. Place the roast on the spit of your barbecue rotisserie. Brush the outside with the basting sauce. Roast over medium-hot coals until the meat thermometer registers 145° (rare) to 175° (well done). Baste occasionally with the sauce.

When the meat is cooked, remove it to a large platter and garnish with the cinnamon apples and spiced peach halves, if desired. Makes 8 servings.

Cinnamon Apples

  1 package (4 oz.) hot cinnamon candies
  1 cup water
12 small apples, peeled, but not cored

Combine cinnamon candies with water in a saucepan; simmer 10 minutes or until medium-thick syrup forms, stirring occasionally. Poach apples in the syrup until tender and rosy red, about 30 minutes. Drain on waxed paper and use to garnish the roast venison.

Ripple-Skewered Venison Steak Sandwiches
SKEWER-COOKED

For best flavor and texture, serve the prime cuts of venison rare or medium-rare.

1¾ to 2-pound good quality venison steak
    (about 1½ inches thick)
  1 cup rosé or dry white wine
    (or 1 cup regular strength beef broth)
  2 tablespoons lemon juice
  1 tablespoon honey
  1 teaspoon seasoned salt
    Few drops liquid hot-pepper seasoning
½ cup catsup
  6 French rolls or frankfurter buns
    Chopped green onion

Cut steak across the grain into diagonal strips about ½ inch wide. Combine the wine, lemon juice, honey, seasoned salt, and hot-pepper seasoning. Pour over meat, and marinate several hours or overnight. Drain meat well, saving marinade. Thread steak strips onto skewers, ripple fashion; grill, close to the barbecue coals until rare or medium-rare. In the meantime, add the catsup to the remaining drained marinade; heat to boiling. Heat or toast 6 split and buttered French rolls or buns. Slip venison strips from skewers into rolls. Spoon hot sauce over meat and sprinkle generously with chopped green onion. Makes 6 servings.

POULTRY

Poultry is so versatile on the barbecue that it is a close second to beef in popularity. To be perfectly cooked, all poultry should be lightly browned outside, tender and juicy inside. Differences in flavors do suggest individual treatment, though.

For grill cooking, choose small birds (such as Cornish game hens, small fryer chickens) split down the back and opened flat. Broiler-fryer chickens can also be cut in halves, quarters, or pieces. Ducklings and turkey pieces will do well on the grill.

Turkey lends itself particularly to smoke-cooking.

Goose and duck (especially domestic varieties) tend to be quite a bit fatter than other poultry. When barbecuing either one, puncture the skin often with a fork to release fat. (You can save drippings for sauce or gravy by placing a shallow drip pan made of foil under the cooking bird.) The outside will be pleasantly crusted and the inside moist.

Any whole bird, and halved plump birds, can be spit-roasted with delicious results.

Spicy Yogurt Chicken
GRILL-COOKED

This marinade and baste for chicken was inspired by the East Indian countries. Use it for grilled chicken quarters or spit-roasted whole chickens.

    2 broiler-fryer chickens (2 to 3 lbs. *each*)
    1 pint (2 cups) plain yogurt
    1 clove garlic, crushed
    1 teaspoon ground ginger
    1 teaspoon chile powder
    1 teaspoon cardamom
    ½ teaspoon ground cloves
    ½ teaspoon ground cinnamon
    2 teaspoons salt
    4 bay leaves, ground or crushed

To grill the chickens, cut in quarters and twist wings enough so each wing tip is locked around the back side of its quarter. For spit roasting, truss whole birds; tie or skewer wing tips over breasts, fasten neck skin to backs with a skewer, and tie drumsticks to tails. Combine yogurt with all seasonings. Put chickens in bowl or baking dish; cover with yogurt mixture. Marinate chickens at least 4 hours, or overnight. Remove from marinade and place on greased grill, skin side up. Cook slowly until tender, turning and basting with marinade; or put whole birds on spit and baste as they turn and roast. Cook until meat is tender when pierced. Makes 8 servings.

Indonesian Chicken Appetizers
SKEWER-COOKED

This chicken appetizer is an adaptation of a classic Indonesian entrée. You can do all the advance preparations early in the day and refrigerate the meat until it's time for you or your guests to cook the appetizers.

    2 whole chicken breasts
    1 package (8 oz.) broken walnuts (2 cups)
    ⅔ cup lime juice
    2 tablespoons regular strength chicken broth
    2 green onions, cut up
    2 small cloves garlic, mashed
    ½ teaspoon salt
    1 cup yogurt or commercial sour cream

Cut the uncooked chicken from the bones into bite-sized pieces and set aside. Combine the nuts, lime juice, chicken stock, onions, garlic, and salt in an electric blender and whirl until the nuts are quite fine. Mix ½ cup of this nut mixture with the yogurt or sour cream to serve as a dip with the chicken; chill thoroughly.

Gently coat the pieces of chicken with the remaining nut mixture and refrigerate for 2 to 3 hours. Then string the coated chicken pieces on skewers and refrigerate until you are ready to cook the meat. Grill the chicken about 5 inches from the source of heat for 5 to 7 minutes, turning once. Serve with the yogurt or the sour cream mixture.

Herbed Chicken
GRILL-COOKED

This barbecue baste for chicken is mild, with a hint of Japanese teriyaki flavor.

1 cup Sherry
½ cup salad oil
1 large onion, grated, or 1 tablespoon
    minced dried onions
1 tablespoon Worcestershire
1 teaspoon soy sauce
1 teaspoon lemon juice
1 teaspoon powdered garlic
1 teaspoon whole thyme
1 teaspoon whole oregano
1 teaspoon whole rosemary
1 teaspoon whole marjoram
2 broiler-fryer chickens (about 2½ lbs. *each),*
    cut into quarters or serving-sized pieces

Several hours before barbecuing, mix thoroughly the Sherry, salad oil, onion, Worcestershire, soy sauce, lemon juice, garlic, thyme, oregano, rosemary, and marjoram. About 1 hour before barbecuing, pour sauce over chicken pieces. Grill chicken over low coals about 40 minutes or until tender. Turn frequently and brush with remaining sauce. Makes 8 servings.

Grilled Chicken
GRILL-COOKED

If using halves or quarters, break the hip, knee, and wing joints to keep the bird flat during grilling. Shape the wings akimbo style, bringing the wing tips onto the cut side. Rinse the chicken; pat dry.

Brush the chicken pieces with melted fat or basting sauce. Place the chicken on a greased grill, skin side up, about 6 to 12 inches above coals giving medium heat.

Cook slowly until tender, turning with tongs and basting frequently. Total time will be about 40 minutes. When done, drumstick meat is soft.

Cook chicken breasts quickly over hotter coals (grill temperature should be about 375°). They will be tender after 10 to 12 minutes on each side.

Baste frequently.

Spread Eagle Chicken
GRILL-COOKED

An unusual way to grill a whole chicken is to cut through the length of its back and open the bird out flat.

Allow a 2½-pound broiler-fryer for each 2 or 3 servings. Have your meatman cut through the length of the back of each chicken. Open each chicken out flat, breaking the breastbone so chicken stays flat. Sprinkle each with salt and pepper. Grill over medium-hot coals about 6 inches from heat source for about 45 minutes or until meat is tender when pierced with the tip of a sharp knife; turn occasionally and baste frequently with melted butter. Serve hot or cold. Cut in halves or pieces to serve.

Basic Chicken Bastes

The mild flavor of chicken adapts well to many different marinades, bastes, and sauces. Here are basting sauces designed to complement barbecued chicken. Brush chicken frequently with the baste while cooking and spoon any remaining baste over the cooked chicken just before serving. Each is enough for 1 broiler-fryer chicken.

Lemon-Herb Butter Baste. To ½ cup (¼ lb.) butter, add 1 tablespoon lemon juice, ¼ teaspoon dried fines herbes, and ¼ teaspoon dried whole chervil.

Brown Sugar-Tarragon Vinegar Baste. Combine in a pan 1 cup firmly packed brown sugar, ½ cup tarragon vinegar, and 2 tablespoons butter; bring to a boil just to blend flavors.

Herb Baste. Melt together ¼ cup butter, dash dried whole savory, dash dried whole rosemary, and dash dried whole thyme.

Golden Glaze Baste. Combine ¼ cup melted butter, 3 tablespoons lemon juice, ½ teaspoon paprika, and ¼ teaspoon liquid hot-pepper seasoning.

Teriyaki Baste. Combine and heat together 1 cup soy sauce, ½ cup sugar, ¼ cup salad oil, 2 teaspoons grated fresh ginger, and 1 clove crushed garlic (optional). Baste chicken during last 30 minutes of cooking.

French Dressing Baste. Baste chicken during last 30 minutes of cooking with oil-and-vinegar salad dressing.

Mustard-Honey Baste. Mix ½ cup honey, ¼ cup prepared mustard, 2 tablespoons lemon juice, and 1 teaspoon salt. Baste chicken during last 10 to 15 minutes cooking time.

Spiced Currant Baste. Combine in a pan 1 jar (10 to 12 oz.) currant jelly, 2 tablespoons lemon juice, 1 tablespoon Worcestershire, 1 teaspoon ground allspice, dash salt, dash pepper; bring to a boil to blend flavors. Baste chicken during last 10 to 15 minutes cooking time.

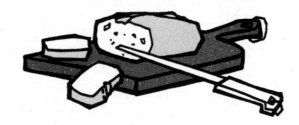

Smoke-Glazed Chicken
SMOKE-COOKED

Cook this chicken in a smoke oven, or in a regular barbecue with any sort of hood over the top to trap the smoke but keep moving ever so slowly through the "chimney." The important thing is to get the chicken well browned and thoroughly cooked.

1 fresh broiler-fryer chicken (2 to 3 lbs.)
2 slices hickory-smoked bacon

Remove the giblets, rinse and dry chicken, and place in a smoke oven. Set a pan of hot coals about 8 inches below the fryer. Lay the 2 strips of good quality hickory-smoked bacon on top of the fryer. To make smoke, occasionally lay on the coals some small pieces of green spicy wood, preferably green apple wood, but green oak or grape is also good.

As the bacon melts, it absorbs smoke from the green wood and forms a glaze on the fryer. As soon as the chicken is rich brown on one side, turn it over and change the bacon again to the top side. About 1¼ hours in a light smoke, with the oven almost closed, produces a flavor quite distinct. (Salt and spices have purposely been omitted because very little of either is needed.) Makes 2 to 4 servings.

Barbecued Chicken, Spanish Style
GRILL-COOKED

Combining barbecued chicken quarters with a colorful rice mixture, this dish is a simple adaptation of the Spanish *arroz con pollo*.

1 large broiler-fryer chicken
  (3 to 3½ lbs.), quartered
½ cup (¼ lb.) butter or margarine
1 clove garlic, minced or mashed
¾ teaspoon salt
¾ teaspoon savory
½ teaspoon paprika
⅛ teaspoon cinnamon
⅛ teaspoon crushed tarragon
  Rice with sausage (recipe follows)

Wash chicken quarters in cool water; pat dry with absorbent material. Melt butter with garlic, salt, savory, paprika, cinnamon, and tarragon. Place chicken quarters on barbecue grill over slowly burning coals; brush frequently with butter mixture, turning occasionally, until chicken is tender and well browned, 40 to 50 minutes. Reserve any remaining butter mixture. Serve chicken atop hot rice-sausage mixture in warm individual casseroles or on a shallow platter. Makes 4 servings.

Rice with Sausage

2 Italian-style pork sausages (½ to 3 oz.
  each) cut into ¼-inch slices
2 medium-sized onions, finely chopped
3 cups cooked rice
1 cup frozen peas, thawed
1 tomato, peeled, seeded, and coarsely
  chopped

Brown pork sausage slices in a frying pan over medium heat. Add onions, and cook until soft and golden. Stir in rice, peas, and tomato. Cover and simmer until thoroughly heated, about 10 minutes; gently blend in any butter mixture reserved after basting the chicken.

Smoked Chicken with Brandy Baste
SMOKE-COOKED

Chicken, cherries, and apricots are brushed with brandy baste and smoked for this dinner entrée.

  Salt
  Pepper
2 broiler-fryer chickens, split
½ cup melted butter
¼ cup lemon juice
¼ cup brandy
¼ cup brown sugar
1 cup fresh (or drained canned)
  dark sweet cherries
12 ripe fresh apricot halves

Salt and pepper chickens. Set on grill over direct heat; cover grill and cook about 40 minutes, basting occasionally with mixture of the butter, lemon juice, brandy, and brown sugar. Place cherries in a shallow pan fashioned of foil; in another pan, put apricot halves, cut side up. Brush fruits with basting sauce. Cook and smoke over direct heat during last 10 minutes that chickens cook. Serve fruit alongside chicken. Makes 4 servings.

Barbecued Breast of Chicken

GRILL-COOKED

This special method of cooking chicken breasts results in tender meat that's juicy and delicious. Success depends on cooking it quickly over hot coals; timing is important.

8 very large chicken breasts
  (almost ½ lb. *each)*, split
  About ¾ cup melted butter
  About 1½ cups flour
  Salt
  Pepper
  About ¼ cup melted butter

Rinse and dry chicken breasts thoroughly. Dip pieces, one at a time, into about ¾ cup melted butter, then shake in a paper bag with flour, seasoned with salt and pepper, to coat thoroughly. Place pieces on a greased grill 6 to 12 inches above hot coals (grill temperature should be about 375°). Cook 10 to 12 minutes on each side. Baste during cooking with about ¼ cup melted butter. Serve immediately. Makes 8 servings.

Pakistani Barbecued Chicken

GRILL-COOKED

Use whole chicken legs and thighs for this quick-cooking chicken entrée—and have the rest of your dinner almost ready before barbecuing the chicken.

For 6 servings, buy 6 whole legs and thighs. With your fingers and a sharp knife, remove skin from each piece and discard. Sprinkle chicken evenly with 1 teaspoon salt, 1½ teaspoons chile powder, and 3 tablespoons lemon juice. Let stand about 30 minutes.

Barbecue until just tender, yet still moist, about 20 minutes. Baste occasionally with ¼ cup melted butter or margarine and turn pieces after about 10 minutes.

Orange-Baked Chicken

COAL-COOKED

Wrap this chicken in foil and place the packets right on the hot coals to cook; cover with more coals. You might also cook skewered vegetables and bake potatoes in the coals.

1 broiler-fryer chicken (2 to 3 lbs.), cut up
  Salt
  Pepper
4 tablespoons frozen concentrated
  orange juice, thawed
4 tablespoons butter

Divide chicken pieces into 4 servings. Sprinkle each serving with salt and pepper, and place it on a piece of heavy duty foil. Pour 1 tablespoon concentrated orange juice over each serving; dot each with 1 tablespoon butter. Wrap foil around each serving of chicken, sealing edges tightly. Bake in hot coals about 1 hour, or until tender. Makes 4 servings.

Lemon-Basted Chicken with Peaches

GRILL-COOKED

Brush the fruit immediately after peeling with the lemon baste to prevent it from darkening. Grill the fruit just long enough to heat it through; two large spoons make the pieces easier to turn without mashing.

2 small broiler-fryer chickens (about 2 to 2½
  lbs. *each)*, cut in half lengthwise
⅓ cup lemon juice
2 tablespoons honey
1 teaspoon salt
6 tablespoons melted butter
4 large freestone peaches or nectarines
  Honey (optional)

Place chickens, cut side up, in a single layer in a pan. Mix together lemon juice, honey, and salt. Pour evenly over chicken; chill, covered, for about an hour. Lift chicken from marinade, draining off juices. Pour marinade into melted butter. Brush chicken with this mixture and place, cut side down, on a grill about 6 inches above medium-hot coals. Allow about 45 minutes cooking time, turning occasionally and brushing with marinade.

Meanwhile, peel, cut in half and pit the peaches or nectarines. Coat with the chicken basting mixture. About 10 minutes before the chicken is done, place fruit, flat side down, on the grill and let heat for 3 or 4 minutes. Turn (use 2 large spoons) onto rounded side and cook about 5 minutes more, brushing with the baste. Serve fruit with chicken. (You can drizzle a little honey over the fruit just before serving if it is not especially sweet.) Makes 4 servings.

Ranch-Style Chicken
GRILL-COOKED

If possible, make the basting sauce for this chicken at least twenty-four hours ahead to blend flavors.

    ½ cup white apple vinegar
    ⅓ cup salad oil
    1½ teaspoons Worcestershire
    ½ teaspoon minced onion
    1 clove garlic, minced
    3 teaspoons salt
    1 teaspoon paprika
    1½ teaspoons tomato paste
    6 to 8 drops liquid hot-pepper seasoning
    ¼ teaspoon dry mustard
    3 broiler-fryer chickens, cut up
    Melted butter

Make the basting sauce by combining the vinegar, salad oil, Worcestershire, onion, garlic, salt, paprika, tomato paste, liquid hot-pepper seasoning, and dry mustard. Brush chicken pieces with melted butter and place over hot coals for about 5 minutes to sear; then turn. Brush chicken with sauce and turn every 3 to 5 minutes, basting with sauce at each turn. Time required is about 35 minutes. Makes 6 servings.

Spit-Roasted Chicken
SPIT-ROASTED

You can spit roast at one time as many chickens as the length of your spit allows.

Rub the cavity or cut side of the chicken lightly with salt. Spoon in stuffing, if used, and close cavity by placing skewers across body opening; lace shut with cord if necessary.

For a whole bird, tie or skewer the wing tips over the breast; fasten the neck skin to the back with a skewer. Push the spit through the bird from the tail end of the bird toward the front so that the point of the spit emerges between the branches of the wishbone. Anchor the chicken to the spit with crossed drumsticks and tail tied together. To spit roast halves, pierce them with the spit through the thigh meat, then the breast meat; anchor. Be

sure the spit prongs are firmly in place and that the bird is balanced on the spit.

Brush the chicken with fat or oil. No further basting is necessary. If you wish, baste the chicken with a seasoned basting sauce several times during the last 20 to 30 minutes of cooking.

Place the chicken over glowing coals; spit-level temperature should be about 400°. Time required will be approximately the same as for oven roasting. When done, the breast meat near the wing joint will be fork-tender; the drumstick meat will be soft.

Buttery Cornish Hens
SMOKE-COOKED

Herb butter, used both inside and outside, blends with a glistening apricot glaze to flavor these juicy Cornish hens. They should be cooked on a barbecue that can be covered; the surface of the grill should be large enough for heat to circulate around the pan holding the hens.

    4 frozen Rock Cornish game hens (12 oz.
        to 1 lb each), thawed
        Salt and pepper
        Herb butter (recipe follows)
    2 tablespoons lemon juice
    ¼ cup warm, strained apricot jam
        Watercress sprigs and fresh apricot
        halves, for garnish

Wash Cornish hens, pat dry, inside and out, with absorbent material. Sprinkle skin and cavities lightly with salt and pepper. Place about 1 tablespoon of the herb butter in large cavity of each; fasten cavities with wooden picks or small metal skewers. Tie legs together.

Melt remaining herb butter with lemon juice. Place hens, breasts up, on a double thickness of heavy foil; turn up a 1-inch rim on all 4 sides to form a shallow pan. Place on grill over glowing coals. Cover barbecue, adjust drafts to keep fire burning slowly, and cook, basting occasionally with herb butter, for 45 minutes to 1 hour or until tender and golden brown.

When almost done, brush hens evenly with warm apricot jam; cover again and continue cooking until nicely glazed. Serve on wooden board or platter, garnished with watercress and apricots. Makes 4 servings.

Herb Butter

To make herb butter, blend ½ cup (¼ lb.) soft butter or margarine with 2 tablespoons chopped chives (fresh or freeze-dried) and ¼ teaspoon rosemary, crushed.

Smoky Turkey with Fruit Dressing
SMOKE-COOKED

For an unusual way to prepare turkey, marinate it, stuff it with a fruit dressing, and then smoke it.

  1 hen turkey (12 lbs.)
  ½ cup soy sauce
  ¼ cup honey
  ¼ cup Sherry
  1 tablespoon grated fresh ginger root
  3 cloves garlic

Marinate the turkey overnight in a mixture of the soy sauce, honey, Sherry, ginger, and garlic.

Stuff turkey lightly (recipe follows), and skewer openings closed. Truss with string, and make a double loop at the drumstick end so that you can hang the bird from a hook.

Build a small fire in a smoke oven, using charcoal and fruitwood, and place bird on hook in chimney. Smoke-cook at a temperature between 300° and 350° until the meat thermometer registers 180°, or approximately 5 to 5½ hours for a 12-pound bird. (Figure about 25 per cent longer than for oven roasting at 325°.)

Fruit Stuffing

  4 tart apples, quartered (unpeeled)
  ½ cup water
  ¼ cup brown sugar
  1 cup cooked, pitted dried prunes
  1½ cups cooked, mixed dried fruits
      (apricots, pears, peaches)
  ¼ teaspoon ground cinnamon
  ¼ teaspoon ground nutmeg
  ¼ teaspoon ground mace
  ½ cup dry Sherry

To make the stuffing, simmer apples in water and brown sugar until barely tender. Add prunes, mixed fruits, cinnamon, nutmeg, mace, and Sherry.

Spit-Roasted Turkey
SPIT-ROASTED

Brush the inside of the bird with basting sauce or sprinkle lightly with salt. It is best to cook the stuffing separately.

Start the barbecue fire early to have briquets burning evenly for a low, steady heat. Arrange the well ignited briquets at the back of the firebox.

Place a drip pan in front of the coals. You can make your own disposable drip pan by folding a double thickness of 18-inch heavy foil into a pan shape.

Insert the spit rod into the center of the neck skin; run it through the body cavity parallel to the backbone. Bring the rod out just above the tail. Insert the spit fork into the breast and the other fork into the tail. Tighten the screws wih pliers.

Tie twine around the turkey to hold the wings close to the body. Tie the tail and legs together in the back of the spit so that the thighs are not pressed against the body and the dark meat will cook faster.

Check the turkey for balance by rotating the spit between the palms of the hands.

Insert a thermometer into the thickest portion of the thigh, being careful that it does not touch a bone.

Attach the spit and brush the turkey with melted butter or salad oil. Start the motor as directed by the barbecue manufacturer.

Baste occasionally, adding drippings from the pan to the basting mixture while barbecuing. If you use a barbecue sauce, brush it on the bird only during the last 30 to 40 minutes of cooking.

Turkey is done when thermometer in the thigh registers 185°. Time required will be approximately the same as for oven roasting.

A boned turkey roll or a turkey breast, which has been boned and tied as a roast, can be barbecued on a spit or in a covered smoke cooker. Thaw the frozen roll first by letting it stand at room temperature overnight.

To cook on a spit, place over medium coals and cook about 37 minutes per pound. To cook in a smoke cooker, place meat on grill over low coals (without smoke chips); put cover on cooker and make draft openings small to keep temperature consistently low. Allow about 35 minutes per pound. It is best to use a roasting thermometer; insert it in the thickest part of the roast before barbecuing and cook until it reaches a temperature of 170° to 175°.

Teriyaki Turkey Roll
SMOKE-COOKED

This turkey roll is marinated in a teriyaki sauce and roasted in a covered barbecue. The meat takes on a shiny dark surface and a rich smoke-teriyaki flavor. Plan to start marinating the turkey roll 24 hours before you smoke-cook it.

1 cup soy sauce
1 cup Sherry
½ cup honey
6 cloves garlic, peeled and halved
¼ cup grated fresh ginger
1 turkey roll (about 3 lbs.)

Combine the soy sauce, Sherry, honey, garlic, and fresh ginger. Pour this marinade over the turkey roll; cover and marinate for 24 hours, turning the meat 3 or 4 times.

Start the fire 30 minutes to an hour before you start cooking. Follow directions given by the manufacturer of your barbecue for starting the fire and maintaining low even heat. Insert a meat thermometer into the center of the turkey roll and place in the center of the grill. Close the lid of the barbecue. Baste the meat with the marinade 2 or 3 times while cooking. You may want to use a grill thermometer if your barbecue doesn't have one; keep the heat regulated between 300° and 350°. Cook for about 2 hours, or until meat thermometer registers about 185°. Makes 6 servings.

Smoked Turkey
SMOKE-COOKED

Turkey is one of the meats most enhanced by smoke flavor, and smoking gives you an exceptionally well-flavored and beautifully browned turkey.

You will need a barbecue with a cover, but if your barbecue is of the brazier type, construct a foil dome to cover it (see page 14). Such a dome will accommodate the largest turkey you can buy. A drip pan is needed, and this can also be made of foil.

Arrange 20 briquets on each side of the drip pan (if you have pre-soaked briquets to start the fire, place 5 of them on the bottom of each charcoal pile).

Start the two charcoal piles at the same time, 30 to 45 minutes before you plant to start the turkey (the briquets should burn down to an even gray color).

Prepare and stuff the turkey exactly as you would for oven roasting. Cooking time will be about the same as for oven roasting, but because the heat is more difficult to control, it is especially helpful to use a meat thermometer for judging how fast the turkey is cooking and when it is done. Set the turkey on the grill with a strip of foil about 5 inches wide directly under its back and with the turkey centered over drip pan.

Place cover on barbecue; if using a foil hood, open two small draft holes on opposite sides of the hood by unfolding seams to about 1 inch above the base ring—this will be your means of regulating the heat of the oven as your turkey roasts. Open the drafts wider to raise the heat, close them more to slow the heat. At the end of each hour, add 6 or 8 briquets to each side.

You'll also find it worthwhile to add wood chips or green wood to your fire to create smoke for flavor. Use any of the prepared wood chips, shavings, or sawdust (usually available wherever briquets are sold). Soak them in water at least 30 minutes before using. Or you can use green woods such as a hickory, oak, or apple. Don't use soft woods that give off resinous smoke, such as pine.

After you have a bed of glowing charcoal, simply top it with a thin layer of the green wood or handfuls of the soaked dry wood. For subtle smoke flavor, add it 1 to 2 hours before the turkey is done; for more pronounced flavor, use it during the entire roasting time.

Duckling with Orange Baste
SPIT-ROASTED

This orange baste enhances the flavor of duckling whether it's barbecued or oven-roasted.

1 duckling (4 to 5 lbs.)
½ cup orange juice
¼ cup soy sauce
1 teaspoon honey
⅛ teaspoon pepper

Truss duckling compactly and spit it from just in front of the tail (through the bone), diagonally to a point near the apex of the wishbone (again through the bone). Spit-roast the duckling 1½ to 2 hours over a medium to low barbecue fire. Baste frequently with orange sauce:

To make sauce, combine orange juice, soy sauce, honey, and pepper. Heat on the side of the grill and brush it warm on the bird. Using poultry shears, cut duckling into quarters to serve. Makes 4 servings.

Orange Barbecued Duckling
GRILL-COOKED

A veteran outdoor chef devised this method of cooking duck outdoors; the recipe is a combination of cooking in foil and browning over the fire.

To Cook the Duckling

Remove giblets. (If you wish, cook giblets and add the cooking stock and giblets to the gravy.) Wash duckling and dry well. Sprinkle about 1 teaspoon salt and ⅛ teaspoon pepper inside cavities. Fill body cavity with orange stuffing (recipe follows; if any is left over, put into a saucepan to use later). Fold neck skin back, but do not truss bird with pins or skewers that might puncture the foil. Arrange the orange slices all over the outside skin.

Have ready a double-thick sheet of heavy foil; if necessary, put two pieces together by folding edges over twice (drugstore fold). Wrap the bird and seal the foil tightly—it is important to contain all the cooking juices. Put on grill over a fairly hot fire. Turn over every 10 minutes; cook about 1 hour to 1 hour 20 minutes.

Remove foil package to a utility pan and cool slightly. Unwrap, saving all the juices. Discard foil and orange on outside of duckling. Spoon stuffing into the saucepan. With poultry scissors, cut duckling in half and put back onto the grill. Cook, turning as needed, until the skin is crisp and brown and the duckling fully tender. Cook the orange stuffing a few minutes more, if needed; season to taste with butter, salt, and pepper, and serve with the duck. Each duckling makes about 2 servings.

Orange-Celery Stuffing

For each duckling, select 1 large, thin-skinned orange. Slice off and discard both ends of the orange; with a thin sharp knife, cut orange in thin slices. Set aside about half the slices to use on outside of duckling. Chop the rest of the orange and put into a bowl. Slice and add 3 large stalks celery, 1 small onion, thinly sliced, and ¼ teaspoon thyme. Mix well. Makes enough for 1 large domestic duck.

Orange Gravy

Pour the drippings collected in the utility pan into a small pan; skim off most of the fat. Add giblet stock or canned chicken broth to make about 1½ cups. Blend 2 tablespoons all-purpose flour with 2 tablespoons Sherry or water; stir into drippings. Add chopped cooked giblets, if you wish. Cook, stirring until thickened. Salt and pepper to taste.

Surprised Squab
SMOKE-COOKED

This recipe utilizes traditional Chinese ingredients to develop a dish that is unusual and tantalizing, but not too exotic for most tastes. Serve it on the patio, where your guests can feel more free about wresting the succulent meat from this bird's multitude of tiny bones.

4 squabs (or Rock Cornish game hens)
3 tablespoons soy sauce
1 tablespoon brown sugar
3 tablespoons Scotch whisky
  Salt and pepper to taste
1 medium-sized onion, chopped
4 squab gizzards, sliced
3 tablespoons butter
2 cups diced white bread
3 medium-sized cooked shrimp or 6 dried
  Chinese shrimp, broken in small pieces
6 water chestnuts, sliced
1 cup milk
1 teaspoon salt
¼ teaspoon pepper
  Salad oil

Marinate the squabs in a mixture of the soy sauce, brown sugar, whisky, salt, and pepper for about 1 hour. Brush the inside and outside of each bird with this mixture several times during the hour.

Fry the onion and gizzards in 1 tablespoon of the butter until brown. Add the remaining 2 tablespoons of melted butter and mix with the diced bread, shrimp, water chestnuts, milk, salt, and pepper. Spoon this stuffing inside each bird, and skewer skin to cover the openings. Skewer together each pair of legs or tie with light wire. Brush skin with oil and hang in a moderate (300° to 400°) Chinese smoke oven for about 1 hour and 15 minutes. Brush the skin with salad oil once again during the cooking process. Serve 1 juicy squab per person.

Duckling with Raisin Sauce
SMOKE-COOKED

This elegant barbecued duck with a wine and golden raisin sauce will serve 2 or 3 people. Brown the duck first to remove most of the fat; then wrap it in foil to finish cooking.

4½ to 5-pound duckling
  2 stalks celery, coarsely sliced (include tops)
  3 sprigs parsley
  ½ lemon, thinly sliced
  4 teaspoons flour
  ¼ teaspoon pepper
  2 tablespoons soy sauce
  2 cups dry white wine or 1 cup *each* wine
    and chicken broth
  1 bay leaf
  ¾ cup golden raisins

Place a foil pan about the same size as the duckling on firebed of a barbecue that has a cover; arrange charcoal around pan, ignite, and let burn until coals are glowing. Wash duckling in cool water; dry with absorbent material. Place celery, parsley, and lemon in large cavity; close cavity with wooden picks or small metal skewers, and tie legs together.

Place duckling, breast up, on grill over foil drip pan; cover barbecue, adjust drafts to keep fire burning slowly, and cook for about 1½ hours or until duckling is well browned. Remove duckling, and discard drip pan and fat; spread coals into center.

Center duckling on a double thickness of heavy foil large enough to completely enclose it; turn sides up slightly while you add the remaining ingredients.

Blend flour, pepper, and soy sauce; stir in wine. Pour wine mixture over duckling. Top with bay leaf and raisins. Enclose duckling in foil, sealing top and ends.

Return foil-wrapped duckling to barbecue, adding more charcoal if needed. Cover barbecue again, and continue cooking over slowly burning coals for 1 hour longer. To serve, unwrap carefully and place duckling on a warm platter or serving board; remove celery, parsley, and lemon from cavity and discard. Pour raisin sauce from foil and serve separately to spoon over duckling. Makes 2 or 3 servings.

Kamo No Koma-Giri
SKEWER-COOKED

These ground duckling meatballs—delicious either as a main dish or as hors d'oeuvres—may seem like a lot of trouble, but the result is worth it. You can alternate the balls on skewers with wedges of unpeeled apple dipped in melted butter.

1 duckling (4 to 5 lbs.)
3 tablespoons soy sauce
1 tablespoon sake or Sherry

Grind the meat from the uncooked duckling; it will yield about 1½ pounds ground meat. Mix the ground duckling with soy sauce and sake or Sherry until thoroughly blended. Chill about 1 hour, or until mixture is stiff enough to handle. Form into balls about 1 inch in diameter and thread on thin wooden or metal skewers. Flatten balls slightly, then grill over hot coals until brown on both sides. (Brown the balls well on one side before you turn them over, so they won't fall off the skewers.) Makes 4 servings as a main dish, 8 to 10 as hors d'oeuvres.

Pheasant Barbecue
GRILL-COOKED

Serve charcoal-broiled pheasant with an orange and watercress salad.

Split young, hung birds in half, brush on both sides with melted butter, and sprinkle with salt and pepper. Grill over hot coals, starting wtih skin side up. Brush occasionally with butter, and turn after 10 minutes. Continue broiling and basting for another 10 to 25 minutes, depending on size of the bird. To avoid dryness, do not overcook pheasant.

Spit-Roasted Wild Duck
SPIT-ROASTED

Pluck and clean wild duck as soon as possible after the "shoot." Plucking is usually preferred to skinning because the skin adds much to flavor and appearance. A blowtorch will help you to remove the last stubborn feathers.

Wild duck is not usually stuffed; however, a slice of onion, a rib of celery, and a piece of apple may be put into the cavity. If you prefer, use instead a sprig of parsley and 2 or 3 juniper berries. Skewer body cavities closed.

Balance the duck on a spit and rub with butter. Roast over hot charcoal for 12 to 25 minutes, depending on how well done you wish the meat. Duck on the rare side will be tenderer, juicier, and more flavorful.

If a crisp skin is desired, pour a little heated brandy over each duck when it is done and allow to flame, or stop the spit and let the fat drip into the fire and flare. Add salt and pepper.

Turkey Parts
in Blue Cheese Sauce
SMOKE-COOKED

Either turkey legs and thighs or turkey breasts are juicy and tender when cooked in a foil pan on a covered barbecue. A thick blue cheese sauce coats the meat and absorbs a mild smoke flavor.

1 cup (½ pt.) cottage cheese
2 ounces blue cheese
¼ cup chopped parsley
¼ cup butter or margarine
½ teaspoon salt
1 small clove garlic, crushed

Buy a split turkey breast (half breast of about a 14-lb. turkey), or a pair of turkey legs and thighs, or buy a whole turkey and have it cut up and freeze the parts you don't barbecue. Shape a pan of double-thick heavy foil to just fit around the turkey parts, securing the corners to prevent sauce from leaking out (or use a foil cake pan). Cover the bottom of the pan with some of the blue cheese sauce. Arrange turkey in the pan, then spread the rest of the sauce over the top to coat the meat completely. Set pan in a hooded barbecue. Cover barbecue and cook slowly for about 1 hour and 45 minutes, or until tender. No basting is needed. Serve with some of the juices collected in the foil pan. Makes about 4 servings.

Blue Cheese Sauce

Combine in an electric blender the cottage cheese, blue cheese, parsley, butter or margarine, salt, and garlic. Whirl until smooth. You can do this ahead; refrigerate until needed.

Pheasant with Cashew Stuffing
SPIT-ROASTED

If the pheasant is frozen and was not hung beforehand, you can do this after thawing, as it will make a big difference in the meat's tenderness. "Hanging" the pheasant simply means letting it age (well wrapped) at room temperature for two days, or in the refrigerator for four days.

1 young pheasant (2½ to 3 lbs.), hung
1 cup coarsely chopped cashew nuts
1 cup chicken broth
4 slices bacon, cooked and chopped
2 tablespoons butter
½ teaspoon salt
   Dash pepper
3 slices bacon

Carefully wipe out the inside of the pheasant with a damp cloth. Stuff with this dressing: Simmer cashew nuts in chicken broth until tender and liquid is absorbed. Mix in the 4 slices of cooked and chopped bacon, the butter, salt, and pepper. Stuff pheasant, truss, and tie 3 slices of bacon over the breast. Impale with spit and roast over medium-hot coals for 50 to 60 minutes, depending on size of the bird. Makes 2 servings.

Crisp-Roasted Goose
SPIT-ROASTED

Buy a small (6 to 9 lbs.) goose. If the goose has been frozen, be sure it is completely thawed, and dried thoroughly. Rub the inside with salt and a cut half of lemon.

Spit the goose, securing it firmly. Roast over medium coals for 1¾ to 2½ hours, or until it is fork tender and the skin is crisp (about 2¼ hours is long enough for a 6 to 7-pound goose).

Broiled Mallard Duck
GRILL-COOKED

Split down the back and then pressed out flat, this duck is cooked in a hinged wire broiler.

1 mallard duck (2 to 3½ lbs.)
1 cup prepared French dressing
1 teaspoon dry mustard
2 teaspoons Worcestershire
2 teaspoons grated orange peel
1 teaspoon grated lemon peel

Split duck down backbone with poultry shears. Place, breast side down, on meat cutting board and break down breast bones by pressing with another board or by pounding gently with a meat tenderizing mallet.

Mix together the French dressing, mustard, Worcestershire, orange and lemon peels; use mixture to baste the duck liberally. Place duck in a hinged wire broiler and grill over hot coals until done to taste (7 to 10 minutes each side), basting it at least once more while cooking. Divide duck at breastbone into two portions and serve. Makes 2 servings.

FISH AND SHELLFISH

Fish that are moderately fat and full-flavored are the best to barbecue, for the smoky flavor accents their own flavor. Salmon, trout, albacore, barracuda, mackerel, rockfish, sablefish (black cod), sturgeon, and striped bass are all excellent for barbecuing.

Serving-sized steaks, fillets, or small whole fish are easiest to handle if held inside a hinged wire broiler, then placed over the barbecue fire. Thicker steaks or fillets may be placed directly on a greased grill. Some whole fish also barbecue well; however, they need special care.

All fish need frequent basting while on the barbecue. In the absence of a specific baste, use melted butter, plus a little lemon juice.

Since fish cooks so quickly on the barbecue, you need to watch it carefully in order not to overcook it. Fish is done when it flakes easily upon testing with a fork. Shellfish requires very little cooking and is done when it becomes less translucent and more opaque.

Bercy Sauce

This sauce is good with most fish—baked, broiled, or barbecued.

Melt 3 tablespoons butter in a pan; add 2 teaspoons minced shallots or green onions and cook until translucent. Stir in 2 tablespoons flour, and cook 1 minute. Then stir in 1 cup fish stock (or substitute ½ cup chicken stock, ½ cup dry white wine). Season to taste with salt and pepper, and at the last, stir in 1 teaspoon minced parsley. Makes about 1¼ cups.

Salmon with Lemon Rice Stuffing
SMOKE-COOKED

If you don't have a covered barbecue, wrap the salmon in foil and turn it from side to side as it cooks.

Fill the cavity of a 3 to 8-pound salmon with the lemon rice stuffing (recipe follows). Sew the opening closed with a heavy thread (any stuffing that doesn't fit into the fish can be wrapped in foil and heated on the grill while the fish cooks). If your barbecue has a hood, shape a piece of heavy foil to fit around bottom of fish; grease the foil. Cut very thin slices from a small, thin-skinned grapefruit; place slices against skin on both sides of fish; then set fish on greased foil. Put on grill over low heat; cover grill. Baste with a little melted butter several times while fish cooks. If your grill doesn't have a hood, wrap the grapefruit-covered fish in double-thick foil. Set it over slowly burning coals (or set the grill as high as possible above coals), and turn about every 10 minutes. Time required is usually about 1 hour. A 4-pound salmon makes about 8 servings.

Lemon Rice Stuffing

Heat ⅓ cup butter or margarine in a frying pan. Add 1 cup sliced celery, 1 small onion (chopped), and 1 to 2 cups sliced fresh mushrooms (optional); sauté about 5 minutes. Add ¼ teaspoon thyme, 1½ teaspoons salt, ⅛ teaspoon pepper, 2 teaspoons grated lemon peel, ¼ cup lemon juice, and 1⅓ cups water. Bring to a boil. Mix in 1¾ cups packaged precooked rice and cover; remove from heat; let stand 5 minutes. Makes enough for an 8-pound fish.

Smoked Fresh Salmon Fillet
SMOKE-COOKED

The rich meat of salmon is especially delicious smoked, and you can smoke a fresh fillet on your barbecue grill in two hours.

Place a 1-pound piece of fresh salmon fillet on a sheet of heavy foil cut to fit the fillet; place on grill over charcoal arranged for indirect heat (high above the coals). Keep temperature low (not over 275°), cover the grill, and smoke (adding wood as needed) for 2 hours. Salt to taste. Use for hors d'oeuvres, sandwiches, or entrées. Makes 20 generous canapés of salmon on buttered bread, or 4 entrées.

Soy-Grilled Albacore Steaks
GRILL-COOKED

Firm, meaty slices of fresh albacore are an excellent choice for barbecuing. If your fish dealer doesn't carry the white-fleshed tuna regularly in the summer, ask him to order one for you.

   4 to 6 albacore steaks
⅓ cup soy sauce
⅓ cup salad oil
   2 cloves garlic, minced or mashed
   2 teaspoons meat seasoning sauce
   2 teaspoons Worcestershire

Ask your dealer to clean and dress the albacore and cut it into steaks about 1 inch thick. At home, cut the dark meat and bone from each steak, leaving skin intact. Press pieces together (don't be concerned if meat seems soft — it firms quickly over heat) and secure with several picks.

   Combine the soy sauce, oil, garlic, meat sauce, and Worcestershire, and pour over prepared steaks. Marinate for 20 to 30 minutes, remove from marinade, and place on a greased grill over medium-hot coals for 10 to 15 minutes, turning once and brushing often with marinade. Makes 4 to 6 servings.

Barbecued Lean White Fish
GRILL-COOKED

You can barbecue thick boneless pieces of any firm-fleshed, lean white fish using this method. Some examples are: halibut, rockfish, lingcod, giant sea bass (black sea bass), white seabass, and totuava.

Cut 4-pound fillet of firm, white fish into pieces about 1 inch wide, 2 inches long, and 1 inch thick. Combine ½ cup soy sauce, 1 cup dry white wine, 2 tablespoons lemon juice, 2 cloves garlic (crushed), 1 teaspoon powdered ginger, and ½ cup salad oil. Pour over fish pieces and marinate 4 hours. Pour off marinade and reserve. Sprinkle fish pieces generously with about 2 tablespoons fresh rosemary and about 6 tablespoons fresh chopped parsley. Skewer carefully or slip inside a hinged wire broiler and place on the grill over low coals. Cook until fish flakes when tested with a fork, about 10 to 15 minutes, basting occasionally with part of the marinade.

   In the meantime, sauté 1 pound sliced fresh mushrooms in ⅓ cup butter; add remaining marinade, heat through, and pour over broiled fish. Makes 8 servings.

Boned Mackerel in Crumb Crust
GRILL-COOKED

The most popular mackerel, the Pacific mackerel (often called blue or American mackerel) is a member of the tuna family. Its dark meat is moderately high in fat content and pronounced in flavor. It's easiest to barbecue if you have it split and boned at the market.

½ cup dry bread crumbs
½ cup grated Parmesan cheese
   2 cloves garlic, crushed
¼ teaspoon salt
   Dash pepper
⅓ cup salad oil
⅓ cup lemon juice
   1 tablespoon chopped parsley
½ teaspoon whole dried basil
   4 mackerels (about 1 lb. each),
      split and boned

Mix dry crumbs with Parmesan cheese, 1 clove of the garlic, the salt, and pepper. Also have ready a basting sauce made by combining salad oil and lemon juice with the remaining 1 clove garlic, chopped parsley, and basil. Dip each fish fillet in the basting sauce, then in crumb mixture. Set over slow coals on a greased grill. Cook slowly, turning once and basting often, until fish flakes (about 15 minutes). Makes 4 servings.

Basic Fish Sauces

For all of these fish sauces, you will find suggestions of the fish each best complements. The sauces may be served at once or refrigerated.

Hollandaise Sauces

For these two sauces you make Hollandaise in a blender, then add either chopped cucumber or shrimp. Serve warm or rewarm them over hot water.

Sauce Hollandaise with Cucumber (salmon, halibut, trout, albacore). Combine in the blender 3 egg yolks (at room temperature) and 1½ tablespoons lemon juice. Melt ¾ cup butter or margarine and heat until it bubbles — don't brown. Add 1 tablespoon hot water to the egg, turn blender on high speed, and immediately pour in hot butter in a steady stream (takes about 5 seconds). Add 1 teaspoon prepared mustard and ½ teaspoon salt and whirl until blended, about 30 seconds. Turn into a bowl and stir in 1 tablespoon each chopped parsley and chives. Peel 1 cucumber, cut in half, scrape out large seeds, chop, and stir into sauce. Makes about 2 cups.

Sauce Hollandaise with Shrimp (salmon, sole, halibut, sea bass, rockfish). Prepare as for Sauce Hollandaise, above, except omit salt; turn into a bowl, omit cucumber, and stir in 1 can (about 5 oz.) shrimp, which have been rinsed and drained.

Mayonnaise Sauces

Mayonnaise is the base of a number of cold fish sauces. Use them on sautéed, broiled, or barbecued fish — served cold on the sizzling hot fish — or on chilled, poached fish.

Here is an easy way to make mayonnaise sauces with a wire whip and round-bottomed bowl or your electric mixer. (If you happen to add oil too fast, causing the mayonnaise to separate, start again with 1 egg yolk in a clean bowl and slowly beat in curdled mixture.)

Herb Mayonnaise Sauce (for any fish). Put into the bowl 2 egg yolks, ½ teaspoon *each* dry mustard, salt, thyme, and tarragon, dash cayenne, 2 tablespoons chopped parsley, 1 tablespoon chopped chives, and 2 tablespoons lemon juice; beat until blended. Measure 1 cup salad oil (may be all or part olive oil); slowly add the oil (about 1 tablespoon at a time), beating constantly. As the mixture begins to get thick, you can beat in the oil more rapidly — in a slow stream. Beat in about 1 tablespoon

hot water to make a good sauce consistency. Makes about 1½ cups.

Brown Butter Almond Sauce (any fish, but best with salmon, halibut, trout). Heat 1 cup (½ lb.) butter until it melts and turns a golden brown; cool to lukewarm. Following Herb Mayonnaise recipe above, add mustard and cayenne to egg yolks, but omit the salt, herbs, parsley, and chives, and reduce lemon to 1 tablespoon. Instead of salad oil, beat the browned butter into egg mixture exactly as directed for the mayonnaise, above. Beat in 1 tablespoon dry Sherry with the hot water. Then stir in ½ cup toasted, slivered almonds. If this becomes too stiff, beat in a little more hot water.

Rémoulade Sauce (sole, rockfish, sea bass, halibut, trout). Prepare the Herb Mayonnaise, above, omitting salt, thyme, and chives; add 1 teaspoon anchovy paste and ½ teaspoon chervil to the egg mixture. After all oil has been added (omit water), stir in ¼ cup finely chopped dill pickle, 1 tablespoon chopped capers, and 2 hard-cooked eggs, chopped.

Horseradish Mayonnaise (delicious with barbecued salmon). Combine in the blender ¼ cup lemon juice, ¾ teaspoon salt, ½ teaspoon sugar, and 1 egg; whirl at high speed. With motor running, remove blender top and add 1 cup salad oil in slow, steady stream; continue whirling about 2 minutes. Stir in 3 tablespoons prepared horseradish. Fold in 1 cup commercial sour cream or 1 cup heavy cream, whipped. Serve immediately, or chill before serving. Makes 2½ cups.

Tomato Sauce

The word Portugaise is often used to designate a tomato sauce. A short cut is employed to make this sauce, using canned stewed tomatoes. Its robust flavor is best suited to fish that have assertive flavors themselves.

Portugaise Sauce (halibut, rockfish, sea bass, albacore). Sauté 1 medium-sized onion (chopped) in ¼ cup butter or margarine until soft. Add 1 crushed clove garlic, ½ teaspoon thyme, ¼ teaspoon crushed rosemary, and 1 can (1 lb.) stewed tomatoes (break up tomatoes with spoon). Simmer, uncovered, stirring occasionally, until reduced to about half — takes about 15 minutes. Add salt and pepper to taste.

Barracuda Steaks
GRILL-COOKED

The flavor and texture of barracuda meat is something like dark meat tuna. Relatively strong in flavor, it takes well to robust seasonings and is an excellent fish to barbecue. Have the whole fish dressed at the market; it is easy to cut steaks or pieces from it at home.

Prepare either a lemon, garlic, or teriyaki baste for this fish (see chapter on Sauces and Marinades). Cut barracuda steaks or fillets about ¾ inch thick. Brush well on both sides with the baste (or marinate in a shallow pan about 10 minutes). Set steaks or fillets on the grill on top of a piece of heavy foil (with holes punched in it), or hold the fish pieces in a hinged wire broiler over the fire. Cook over medium-hot coals, turning and basting as needed, for 8 to 10 minutes, or until the fish flakes easily.

How to Grill Fish
GRILL-COOKED

Serving-Sized Steaks, Fillets, and Small Whole Fish. Fairly thick fish steaks or fillets may be placed directly on the greased grill of your barbecue, but smaller fish pieces are easier to handle if held inside a hinged wire broiler.

Cut fish into serving-sized steaks or fillets; they should be at least ½ inch thick. Clean small, whole fish and remove heads, if you wish. Wipe with a damp cloth.

Place fish over moderately hot coals; baste.

Grill, turning once, and basting often until fish is browned and flakes when tested with a fork; time will be about 8 to 16 minutes, depending on thickness. Salt and pepper to taste. Serve at once.

Whole Fish, Five to Seven Pounds. Whole fish, such as barracuda, sablefish (black cod or butterfish), and salmon, may be barbecued easily. Remove the dorsal fin (at center of back) by cutting along either side of fin, then pulling it forward to remove it with root bones attached. This provides a point for inserting a thermometer. Cut off the pectoral fins (just back of gills) without disturbing root bones.

If you wish to keep the head and tail on as you cook, wrap them with oiled waxed paper and then with foil.

Slip fish inside folded strip of expanded aluminum (a wire mesh available at hardware stores) with tail in the fold. Lace side of metal strip together with wire; keep it loose, for fish will expand as it cooks.

Place fish on grill and brush lightly with salad oil. Place foil-covered pieces of wood under head and tail to protect them from heat. Cover with barbecue hood or a large sheet of heavy foil; cook slowly, turning as needed.

Insert thermometer through opening where dorsal fin was removed when you turn fish. Add hickory chips or hardwood to the fire for extra smoke. Fish is done when it flakes when tested with a fork, or reaches about 120° on meat thermometer (120° isn't marked on most meat thermometers, but can be estimated).

Remove fish from grill. Cut wires and fold back top layer of metal strip. Grasp fish and metal strip, pull toward you, and lift on to serving board. Remove foil and top skin, and serve.

Large Fish Fillets. Fillets of albacore, giant sea bass, small halibut, lingcod, rockfish, sablefish, salmon, and white seabass (or totuava) all do well on the barbecue. Have fish cut into fillets (weighing 3 to 5 pounds), leaving skin on. Cut pieces of heavy foil about the same size as the fillets and place against skin side of each fillet; lay on grill, skin sides down. Cover barbecue with lid or blanket of heavy foil and cook over slow coals until fish flakes when tested with a fork. Baste occasionally. (A 3 to 4-pound fillet will take about 25 minutes to cook approximately 1 foot above moderate coals.)

When fish is done, lift each foil-lined fillet to a serving plate or plank. To serve, cut across fillets and just to the skin; lift each serving away from skin. Serve with additional baste or your favorite sauce for fish.

Butterflied Shrimp Appetizers
SKEWER-COOKED

Breaded shrimp, basted with lime or lemon butter, can be barbecued on individual hibachis right at the table.

    1 pound jumbo or medium shrimp
    1 egg
    ¼ teaspoon salt
    ¼ teaspoon pepper
      Fine dry bread crumbs
    ½ cup melted butter
    ¼ cup lime or lemon juice
      Lime wedges

Remove shells, tails, and veins from the shrimp and slit each one down the back side, cutting almost all the way through so it will lie flat (take care not to cut entirely in half). Dip shrimp in egg, slightly beaten with salt and pepper; then dip in bread crumbs to coat each side (you'll need about ½ cup of crumbs).

Thread each shrimp on a skewer. Insert point of skewer at tail of shrimp and impale its full length so that the point of the skewer just shows at the head end. Refrigerate until ready to cook. Cook over hot coals; baste occasionally with a mixture of melted butter and lime or lemon juice. Serve with lime wedges to squeeze over shrimp. Makes about 16 large or 25 medium appetizers.

Fish Smoked in Paper
COAL-COOKED

Fish cooked this way is moist and has a mild smoky flavor; if you have any left over, it's delicious served cold. This is a good way to prepare and carry fish to a picnic site, as the paper will keep the fish cold for several hours. The rest of the picnic menu might be: small pumpernickel bread and butter sandwiches, husk-roasted corn, white wine or lemonade, watermelon, and coffee.

You can use salmon, flounder, or rockfish, allowing about 1 pound per person. For 8 to 10 people, plan on 3 fish of about 3 pounds each, or 2 fish of 4 to 4½ pounds each. You'll need long tongs for turning the fish while cooking, and water to quench any flames.

Clean the fish, removing heads and tails; rub with salt (about 1 teaspoon per pound of fish) and sprinkle with pepper. Stuff the cavity of each fish with equal parts chopped parsley and finely chopped onion. Wrap each fish well in buttered waxed paper, then in several layers of newspaper so there is a 1-inch thickness of paper (you'll need about 8 double sheets of newspaper for a 3-pound fish). To make the packet easier to handle, tie with string.

Dip the packets in water to moisten the outer layer of paper, and place on hot coals (not flames). Let the newspaper smoulder but not flame (quench flames with water). Using long tongs, turn packets over 4 or 5 times in the first half hour and moisten the charred paper. When packets have smoldered down to the waxed paper layer (it takes about 1¼ hours for a fish of about 3 pounds to cook), use tongs to remove from hot coals onto a tray or cooky sheet. Remove the charred newspaper and waxed paper from one side of each fish and turn over onto serving platter; then remove the paper from the other side of each fish. Serve with melted butter and lemon slices.

How to Cook Shellfish
GRILL-COOKED

Shrimp and lobsters are the two shellfish most used in barbecuing.

Shrimp lend themselves especially to skewer cooking, but can be grilled. In either case, watch for the meat to change from translucent to opaque. Remove it from the heat while it is still visibly moist.

Spiny Pacific (or rock) lobsters are easiest to handle if they are first boiled, then cleaned and split for barbecuing; care must be taken only to reheat the meat, not further cook it.

Live Northeastern lobsters may be killed, cleaned, split, then barbecued; this method is not for the squeamish, but it results in the most succulent and tender barbecued lobster.

To clean a cooked lobster, take a sharp knife and split the lobster end to end through the shell. Remove the small sac (stomach), which lies just behind the head, and pull out the intestinal vein, which runs down to the end of the tail. Don't discard the coral colored roe (if any) or the yellow liver. (Beat the roe of one lobster with ¼ to ½ cup butter and serve in place of melted butter.) Twist off and discard spiny lobster legs. Crack claws of Northern lobsters. If you wish to remove all the meat from a spiny lobster at once, grasp tail and body and bend the shell backward at the joint until it breaks.

To Barbecue Cooked Lobster. Spread each half of the split, cleaned lobster with melted butter or whipped seasoned butter; wrap each half in foil and place, shell side down, on a grill over medium heat just until lobster is heated through; this will take about 15 minutes.

To Barbecue Uncooked Northern Lobster. First kill the lobster instantly by holding it on its back and inserting the tip of a sharp knife between the tail section and the body shell, cutting to sever the spinal cord. Split the lobster lengthwise and remove the stomach and intestinal vein as described above.

Place split lobster on a greased grill, meat side down. Barbecue about 4 inches from coals for about 5 minutes. Turn and brush meat generously with melted butter or whipped seasoned butter. Barbecue 5 to 7 minutes longer or until meat is cooked, basting often. Serve with melted butter, lemon butter, or a flavored mayonnaise.

To Barbecue Frozen Lobster Tails. Frozen lobster tails are all of the spiny lobster type; they are usually frozen uncooked and may or may not be in the shell. It is important that they be completely thawed before barbecuing. Barbecue lobster tails as directed above for uncooked Northern lobster.

Fish Steaks with Bran
SMOKE-COOKED

If you like the special flavors that cooking with smoke adds to foods, try this suggestion for fish steaks or fish fillets.

Sprinkle the fish on both sides with salt and pepper, and spread generously with butter. Put in a hinged wire broiler. Have ready a good charcoal fire, and sprinkle it with 2 cups whole bran that you've mixed with 3 tablespoons brown sugar. Put fish over the fire, and cover with the barbecue hood (or make a hood of heavy foil). Grill fish for 3 or 4 minutes, then turn and cook on other side, replacing the hood. (Length of cooking time depends upon the thickness of the fish. Test by flaking with a fork.) If the smoke dies down before the fish is cooked, add more sweetened bran.

Baluk Shish Kebab
SKEWER-COOKED

These Armenian skewered fish cubes should be tender and juicy, so be careful not to overcook them. You can alternate the fish pieces with small canned or parboiled onions if you wish.

2½ pounds salmon or halibut, cut in 1-inch
cubes (leave skin on one side of each cube)
    Salt
    Pepper
    White wine
    Bay leaves
    Olive oil

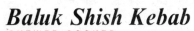

Sprinkle fish cubes with salt and pepper and cover with white wine. Refrigerate for 3 hours, then drain and thread on skewers with half a bay leaf next to each piece of fish. (Be sure to put skewer through the skin on each fish cube.) Brush with olive oil; grill over hot coals 3 to 4 minutes on each side or until the flesh loses its translucent look. Do not overcook. Makes 6 to 8 servings.

Butterflied Trout
GRILL-COOKED

Boned, butterflied trout marinate in Italian-style dressing, and then are barbecued; serve them with nut butter.

Bone 4 medium-sized dressed trout as directed below; place in shallow pan and pour about 1½ cups Italian-style oil and vinegar dressing over fish; allow to stand, covered, in refrigerator about 30 minutes. Remove fish

from marinade; place, skin side down, on barbecue grill. Cook about 10 minutes, or until flesh of trout is white and moist. If you wish, brush occasionally with marinade. Meanwhile, melt ½ cup (¼ lb.) butter or margarine, and add ½ cup chopped salted macadamia nuts; keep warm. Remove trout to heated platter; serve with nut butter. Makes 4 servings.

How to Bone Trout

To bone dressed, uncooked trout and keep the head and tail in place, open the body cavity; insert a sharp knife at the head end under the backbone and cut between ribs and flesh, releasing the bones from the fish back (take care not to cut through the back of the fish). Repeat to free the other side of the backbone and rib cage. Ease backbone free, leaving back flesh of trout intact. Using kitchen scissors, snip backbone at head and tail; lift out bony skeleton and discard. Cut off and discard fins. Fish is now ready for barbecuing open.

Fish with Fennel
GRILL-COOKED

Next time you grill fish outdoors, try this method so popular in Provençe, France.

Use any whole, firm-fleshed fish. Clean, remove head if you wish, and make a few diagonal incisions in both sides. Brush with olive oil and sprinkle with salt and pepper. Lay a few branches of fennel (anise) across the fish on both sides, and fasten in a greased wire hinged broiler. (If you don't have fennel, use thyme, bay leaves, or dill, preferably branches, though the crushed herbs may be sprinkled on.) Grill the fish on both sides, sprinkling a few times with a little more oil. When it's cooked, arrange it on a flameproof platter, sprinkle with brandy, and flame. Serve with lemon wedges and Rémoulade Sauce (see page 74).

Shellfish Kebabs
SKEWER-COOKED

Serve this as an entrée with fried rice, or as hors d'oeuvres with any remaining marinade kept hot in a chafing dish for dunking purposes.

⅓ cup soy sauce
1 medium-sized white onion, chopped
2 tablespoons grated fresh ginger
2 cloves garlic, finely chopped
2 teaspoons dry mustard
1 teaspoon prepared horseradish
½ teaspoon curry powder
2 pounds large shrimp
1 pint medium-sized oysters
½ pound very lean bacon
4 to 6 tomatoes
12 to 16 pearl onions
2 green peppers

Prepare marinade by combining soy sauce, white onion, ginger, garlic, mustard, horseradish, and curry powder. (The marinade can be mixed the night before, allowed to stand overnight in the refrigerator, then brought out about 6 hours before broiling to allow it to come to room temperature.)

Shell and devein shrimp, then marinate at least 2 hours.

Puff oysters slightly in hot water and cook bacon to the limp stage. Then wrap oysters in half slices of bacon, using toothpicks to hold. Cut tomatoes into quarters, leave onions whole, and cut peppers into bite-sized chunks. Impale all ingredients on skewers and grill over a medium-hot charcoal fire for 3 to 5 minutes, or until done to taste, basting frequently with heated marinade during the cooking. Makes 6 to 8 servings as an entrée, at least twice that many for hors d'oeuvres.

Onigari Yaki
SKEWER-COOKED

In this recipe you skewer shrimp to make a fancy serpentine design. Brush with the soy-wine sauce while barbecuing.

½ cup Mirin (Japanese wine) or Sherry
1 cup soy sauce
1 tablespoon sugar
About 3 pounds shrimp

In a small saucepan, combine Mirin or Sherry, soy sauce, and sugar; bring to a boil. Thread 6 medium-sized shrimp or prawns on each of 6 skewers, alternating heads and tails as follows: Thread the head of one shrimp, with the tail curling over top of skewer; then thread the head of another shrimp with the tail curling up from bottom of skewer. Thread the tail of the first shrimp, the head of a third shrimp, then the tail of second shrimp, and so on. Shrimp will be alternately upcurled and downcurled. Cook over hot coals, brushing constantly with sauce until shrimp are shiny and glazed. Makes 6 servings.

Slow-Smoked Garlic Fish
GRILL-COOKED

From June to July (depending upon the weather) until about the end of October, you can buy fresh white fish. The rest of the year, frozen fish is available in most markets.

1½ lemons, very thinly sliced
1 large firm, white fish steak (about 1½ lbs.), cut 1 inch thick
1 large clove garlic, minced or mashed
⅓ cup butter
Salt
Pepper

Place lemon slices over bottom of shallow pan fashioned of heavy foil. Lay fish steaks on lemon. Pour garlic butter (made by heating garlic in butter) over steak. Sprinkle with salt and pepper to taste. Place on grill over indirect very low heat (not over 275°). Cover grill and smoke for 2 hours. Baste with juices in pan. Makes 4 servings.

Fish Kebabs Piraeus
SKEWER-COOKED

Offer traditional Greek seasonings — lemon wedges and a bowl of dried oregano — to sprinkle over these fish kebabs at the table. It's important to marinate the fish overnight so the seasonings have a chance to permeate.

¼ cup salad oil or olive oil
½ cup dry white wine
2 tablespoons lemon juice
1 teaspoon salt
1 teaspoon dried oregano, crumbled
¼ teaspoon garlic salt
1 tablespoon instant minced onion
3 firm, white fish steaks (about 2 pounds),
   cut ¾ inch thick
1 large green pepper
12 bay leaves
12 cherry tomatoes
6 mushroom caps
   (about 1½ inches in diameter)
1 lemon, cut in wedges
   Oregano

For marinade, mix together in a bowl the oil, wine, lemon juice, salt, oregano, garlic salt, and onion. Cut fish steaks into 1¼-inch squares, place in the marinade, cover and chill overnight, turning several times. Cut pepper in half, remove seeds, and cut in 1¼-inch squares.

Compose 6 skewers in the following pattern: alternate 1 piece fish, 1 square of pepper, fish, bay leaf, tomato, fish, bay leaf, tomato, fish, pepper, fish, and end with a mushroom cap.

Barbecue skewers over medium coals for 10 minutes, turning to brown both sides and basting several times with the marinade. Accompany with lemon wedges and a small dish of oregano. Makes 6 servings.

Orange-Soy Fish
GRILL-COOKED

Firm, white, boneless fish holds together well and is easy to manage on the barbecue. To prevent breakage when turning, use kitchen tongs.

½ cup soy sauce
¼ cup catsup
¼ cup chopped parsley
½ cup orange juice
2 cloves garlic, mashed
2 tablespoons lemon juice
1 teaspoon pepper
1½ to 2 pounds firm, white fish,
   cut 1 inch thick

Combine in a bowl the soy sauce, catsup, parsley, orange juice, garlic, lemon juice, and pepper. Mix well. Marinate fish in this mixture for 1 hour. Grill about 4 inches above hot coals for about 8 minutes. Turn fish and grill 7 minutes on other side. Brush with marinade frequently during cooking. Makes 4 servings.

Shrimp and Anchovy Appetizers
SKEWER-COOKED

Jumbo shrimp stuffed with anchovies and wrapped in bacon are elegant appetizers. Plan on at least two for each guest.

Shell jumbo shrimp and split each deeply down the back, removing the sand vein. Insert a fillet of anchovy in each slit; wind with a half-slice of bacon (split bacon lengthwise) and fasten with a pick. Broil over charcoal until the bacon is crisp. Don't overcook if you want these at their best; they should be hot and juicy, never dry.

Spicy Shrimp Appetizers
SKEWER-COOKED

Wash, shell, and devein about 2 pounds medium-sized shrimp or prawns (or use about 1½ pounds frozen deveined large shrimp—they need not be thawed). In a bowl or glass jar, blend 1 teaspoon chile powder with 1 tablespoon vinegar, ¼ teaspoon pepper, 1 clove minced or mashed garlic, 1 teaspoon salt, 1 teaspoon basil, and 1 tablespoon finely chopped fresh mint. Stir in ¾ cup salad oil and shake or mix until well blended. Pour over the shrimp; cover the dish and marinate in the refrigerator for at least 4 hours, or overnight. Thread the shrimp on skewers and grill for 6 to 10 minutes (depending on size), turning once and basting liberally with the marinade. Makes 50 appetizers.

SAUCES AND MARINADES

Barbecuing adds new dimensions to meats, since flavor from the smoke penetrates and accents the natural meat flavors. Complementary marinades, bastes, and sauces add still other dimensions.

The words marinade, baste, and sauce are used somewhat interchangeably. In many cases, this is the truth of the matter. In some cases, they are separate things.

A marinade accomplishes several things when it serves to marinate meat. The acid (from citrus juice, wine, or vinegar) acts as a tenderizer. Fat (from salad oil or melted butter) adds moisture to very lean meats. Seasonings impart interesting flavors. Most of the recipes for marinades are in the recipe chapters because many a true marinade is designed to accompany a specific meat.

A baste is brushed onto meat while cooking, which means that its flavor does not permeate as deeply as a marinade might, unless the same liquid has already served to marinate the meat. In this case, the baste deepens the flavor. The prime role of a baste, however, is to conserve moisture in the meat. Most of the recipes in this chapter are for bastes.

A sauce may be leftover marinade or baste, or may be prepared separately. In any event, it is spooned over the cooked meat upon serving in order to give its own fillip to the flavor of the dish.

A specialized form of the sauce is a seasoned butter. Like a liquid sauce, it is spread over the finished meat rather than applied during the cooking.

The following recipes are for rather widely usable bastes, sauces, and butters. More specialized forms of the subtle complements to your barbecued meat are to be found in each of the separate chapters of recipes.

Purple Plum Baste

Use either fresh plums or canned purple plums for this baste for chicken or pork. If you use canned plums, simply pit and purée. If you use fresh plums, cook 8 to 10 plums with ½ cup water and ⅓ cup sugar until tender, then purée.

1 can (1 lb.) purple plums with syrup
  (or cooked fresh plums), puréed
¼ cup lemon juice or vinegar
2 tablespoons chopped onions
2 tablespoons brown sugar, firmly packed
2 tablespoons salad oil or melted butter
½ teaspoon salt

Combine plum purée, lemon juice or vinegar, onions, sugar, salad oil, and salt. Bring to a boil; simmer 10 to 15 minutes. Makes about 2 cups sauce.

Golden Papaya Baste

The golden color of papaya coats chicken or pork. In places where the baste caramelizes, the papaya flavor becomes even richer.

1 can (9 oz.) undrained sliced papaya,
  puréed (or use mashed fresh fruit
  with 3 tablespoons sugar)
2 tablespoons white wine vinegar
2 tablespoons Sherry or fruit juice
2 tablespoons salad oil or melted butter
1 tablespoon honey
½ teaspoon salt
¼ teaspoon powdered ginger or curry powder

Combine papaya, vinegar, Sherry or fruit juice, salad oil, honey, salt, and ginger or curry powder. Bring to a boil; simmer 10 to 15 minutes. Makes about 1¼ cups.

Sauce Bercy for Grilled Meats

In a saucepan, cook 1 tablespoon minced shallots or green onions in 2 tablespoons butter until soft. Add 1 cup dry white wine; simmer until liquid is reduced by half. Mix together ¼ cup (⅛ lb.) butter and 2 teaspoons flour; add to the liquid in pan. Cook, stirring, until thickened. Stir in 1 tablespoon minced parsley and salt and pepper to taste.

Savory Raisin Baste

This full-flavored, moderately thick baste becomes a crusty glaze on the meat, fruity and slightly sweet-sour in flavor. It's especially good on rare beef steak.

½ cup raisins (or cooked prunes, pitted)
¼ cup chopped onion
 1 small clove garlic, minced or mashed
½ cup catsup
½ cup regular strength beef broth
   or dry white wine
 3 tablespoons salad oil
 2 tablespoons wine vinegar
 1 tablespoon brown sugar, firmly packed
 1 teaspoon prepared mustard
 1 teaspoon liquid smoke
½ teaspoon salt
⅛ teaspoon dill weed

Purée raisins (or chop very fine). Combine with onion, garlic, catsup, broth or wine, salad oil, vinegar, sugar, mustard, liquid smoke, salt, and dill. Simmer 10 to 15 minutes. Makes about 1¾ cups.

Cheddar-Sherry Sauce

Serve Cheddar-Sherry sauce hot over steaks, lamb chops, or any other meats.

¼ pound process Cheddar cheese
½ cup Sherry
 1 teaspoon dry mustard
½ teaspoon seasoned salt
¼ teaspoon paprika
   Salt to taste

Melt cheese in double boiler and add Sherry, a little at a time, stirring constantly. When well blended, add mustard, seasoned salt, paprika, and salt to taste, stirring thoroughly. Serve hot.

Herb Wine Marinade

Here's a marinade for chicken with two variations: one that can be used for lamb, and another for beef or pork.

 1 cup dry white wine
¼ cup lemon juice
 2 tablespoons wine vinegar
 2 cloves garlic, crushed
 1 teaspoon salt
 1 teaspoon dried whole tarragon or rosemary
 2 tablespoons melted butter or salad oil

In a saucepan, combine the wine, lemon juice, vinegar, garlic, salt, tarragon or rosemary, and butter or salad oil; heat just to simmering; remove from heat. Cover and let stand for 1 hour to allow flavors to blend. Pour sauce over broiler-fryer chicken halves or quarters, and let marinate 1 to 4 hours, depending on how thoroughly you wish the flavors to penetrate. Use the remaining sauce to baste the chicken while barbecuing.

Honey-Wine Marinade for Lamb

Omit lemon juice and tarragon or rosemary in recipe above, and add ⅓ cup honey and 1 teaspoon fresh or dried chopped mint. Pour sauce over lamb chops, steaks, shanks, or breast, and let marinate 1 to 4 hours depending on how thoroughly you wish the flavor to penetrate. Use remaining sauce to baste the lamb while barbecuing.

Red Wine Marinade

Use dry red wine in place of the white wine in basic recipe above; omit the lemon juice and tarragon or rosemary. Add 1 teaspoon dried whole oregano or basil. Pour sauce over steak, spareribs, or pork chops, and let marinate 2 to 6 hours, depending on how thoroughly you wish the flavors to penetrate.

Sweet-Sour Pineapple Baste

Brush this over white fish as it grills over the barbecue coals, or try it on other fish, chicken, or spareribs to add moistness and richness.

1 can (8½ oz.) crushed pineapple, undrained
¾ cup regular strength chicken broth
  or dry white dinner wine
3 tablespoons white wine vinegar
2 tablespoons salad oil
1 tablespoon soy sauce
1 tablespoon chopped onion
1 tablespoon brown sugar, firmly packed
1 teaspoon lemon juice
½ teaspoon garlic salt

Combine pineapple, chicken broth or wine, vinegar, salad oil, soy sauce, onion, sugar, lemon juice, and garlic salt. Bring to a boil and simmer 10 to 15 minutes. Makes about 1⅔ cups.

Soy-Ginger Marinade and Baste

This teriyaki-type marinade adds flavor to beef, chicken, spareribs, and fish.

2 tablespoons salad oil
⅓ cup soy sauce
2 tablespoons honey or firmly packed
  brown sugar
1 tablespoon red wine vinegar
1 teaspoon freshly grated ginger
1 clove garlic, crushed

Combine salad oil, soy sauce, honey or brown sugar, vinegar, ginger, and garlic. For beef, marinate 8 hours in this mixture for delicate flavor, overnight for more pronounced flavor. For chicken or spareribs, marinate 4 to 8 hours. For fish (such as shrimp, fish steaks, giant sea bass steaks), marinate 2 to 4 hours. Use the sauce also to brush on meat while grilling.

Three-Way Tomato Relish

This tomato relish is made with three different degrees of spiciness. Each pint gets a little hotter, and you can flavor beef, pork, fowl, and strong-flavored fish with whichever version you choose. The relish keeps in the refrigerator for up to a month, or may be cooled slightly and frozen.

4 pounds medium-sized ripe tomatoes
  (about 12)
3 large onions, peeled and chopped
2 cups white vinegar
2 cups chopped celery
¾ cup sugar
¼ cup prepared horseradish
2 teaspoons salt
2 teaspoons dry mustard
½ teaspoon paprika
2 cloves garlic, minced or mashed
1 teaspoon whole dried basil
2 teaspoons whole mixed pickling spices
2 green peppers, seeded and chopped
3 small dried hot chile peppers, crushed

Peel tomatoes and chop coarsely. Place chopped tomatoes in a large deep pan (at least 5 quarts) with onions, vinegar, celery, sugar, horseradish, salt, mustard, paprika, garlic, and basil, along with the pickling spices (tied in a square of cheesecloth). Bring tomato mixture to a boil, reduce heat, and boil slowly, uncovered, for 1 hour, stirring occasionally. Add green pepper and continue cooking for 1½ hours longer, stirring frequently. Remove seasoning packet and discard it. Ladle ⅓ of the sauce into a clean 1-pint jar. To remaining sauce, add 2 of the dried hot chiles and continue cooking for 15 minutes more; ladle ½ of this mixture into another clean 1-pint jar. Add remaining chile to sauce still in the pan and cook the mixture for 15 minutes before placing in a third jar. Serve at room temperature. Makes 3 pints of sauce.

Bercy Butter for Grilled Meats

For grilled meats, butter is flavored with the ingredients usually found in the creamy Bercy Sauce. It's delicious on barbecued lamb or beef.

Cook 1 tablespoon minced shallots or green onions in ½ cup dry white wine until wine is reduced by half. Cool and add 6 tablespoons butter creamed with 1 tablespoon minced parsley. Add salt and freshly ground black pepper to taste.

Basic Lemon Butter Baste

Use this basic mixture for chicken halves or quarters, or on any kind of fish that you wish to barbecue. Variations are given to use with turkey, lamb, and hamburgers.

½ cup (¼ lb.) butter, melted
¼ cup lemon juice
½ teaspoon salt

Combine the butter, lemon juice, and salt. Brush the baste onto the meat several times during the entire cooking time.

Herb Butter Baste for Chicken or Turkey

Add ¼ teaspoon rosemary and ¼ teaspoon thyme to the melted butter before adding the lemon juice and salt.

Parsley Orange Baste for Lamb

Add 2 tablespoons grated orange peel, 2 tablespoons finely chopped parsley, and 2 tablespoons honey to the butter before adding lemon juice and salt.

Savory Baste for Hamburgers

Add 2 teaspoons brown bottled gravy sauce and ¼ teaspoon pepper to the basic recipe.

Smoky Peach or Apricot Baste

If you use peaches for this baste, try a dash of allspice to bring out the peach flavor. Try the baste first on lamb, but you may also like it on pork or chicken.

1 can (about 9 oz.) peaches or apricots,
    undrained (or use about ½ cup peeled and
    sliced ripe fresh fruit mashed
    with 3 tablespoons sugar)
¼ cup catsup
 3 tablespoons lemon juice
 2 tablespoons salad oil or melted butter
½ teaspoon liquid smoke
½ teaspoon salt
⅛ teaspoon grated lemon peel

Purée fruits. Combine with catsup, lemon juice, salad oil, liquid smoke, salt, and lemon peel. Bring to a boil; simmer 10 to 15 minutes. Makes about 1½ cups.

All-Purpose Barbecue Sauce

This subtle barbecue sauce adds good flavor to meat, fish, or chicken.

¼ cup salad oil
¼ cup bourbon or Sherry
 2 tablespoons soy sauce
 1 teaspoon Worcestershire
 1 teaspoon garlic powder
    Freshly ground black pepper to taste

Combine salad oil, bourbon or Sherry, soy sauce, Worcestershire, garlic powder, and pepper. Pour over meat and marinate in refrigerator (turning occasionally). Marinate roasts 24 to 48 hours; steaks, 4 hours; salmon or chicken, 2 hours. Also use as a basting sauce.

Sauce Potpourri

Use sauce potpourri to baste meat or fish while cooking, or dip slices or chunks of hot cooked meat into the heated sauce before serving.

1 clove garlic, minced
1 small onion, minced
¾ teaspoon dry mustard
1 tablespoon grated fresh horseradish
1 tablespoon mixed minced herbs
    (thyme, marjoram, parsley)
2 tablespoons vinegar
3 cups water
¾ teaspoon salt
1 tablespoon bottled meat sauce
    or Worcestershire
⅔ cup butter
½ cup catsup
½ teaspoon liquid hot-pepper seasoning
 2 teaspoons sugar
¾ teaspoon chile powder
¼ teaspoon freshly ground black pepper

Combine all ingredients and cook slowly for 45 minutes. Makes 3 cups sauce.

Fresh Tomato Barbecue Sauce

Barbecue sauces made with fresh tomatoes are exceptionally good. If you have an abundant supply of home-grown tomatoes, a sauce is a good way to use a large quantity quickly. This sauce freezes well and is a complement to beef, pork, poultry, and strongly flavored fish.

  1 medium-sized onion, chopped
  3 stalks celery, chopped
  3 tablespoons butter or margarine
  2 cups meaty tomatoes, peeled,
    seeds and pulp removed, diced
  ¼ cup salad oil
  ¼ cup cider vinegar
  ¼ cup lemon juice
  6 tablespoons brown sugar, firmly packed
  2 tablespoons prepared mustard
  2 tablespoons Worcestershire
  1 tablespoon salt
  1 tablespoon pepper

Sauté onions and celery in butter over medium heat until translucent. Add tomatoes and cook over medium-low heat for 5 minutes. Add salad oil, vinegar, lemon juice, sugar, mustard, Worcestershire, salt, and pepper; cook for 10 minutes, stirring sauce occasionally. Makes 3 cups.

Sweet-Sour Tomato Barbecue Sauce

With sweet-sour overtones, this rich tomato sauce is good with barbecued ribs (beef or pork), beef steaks, or chicken. Use it as a baste; then heat and serve it with the cooked meat.

  1 medium-sized onion, sliced
  1 green pepper, seeded and sliced
  2 tablespoons butter or salad oil
  1 can (1 lb., 12 oz.) whole tomatoes
  ¼ cup brown sugar, firmly packed
  2 tablespoons white wine vinegar
  1 small can (8¾ oz.) pineapple tidbits
  ½ teaspoon salt
  ½ teaspoon Worcestershire
    Dash pepper
    Dash liquid hot-pepper seasoning
  1 whole lemon, sliced

Sauté onion and pepper in butter just until tender. Add undrained tomatoes, brown sugar, vinegar, pineapple and syrup, salt, Worcestershire, pepper, and liquid hot-pepper seasoning. Simmer, uncovered, about 15 minutes. Add lemon slices and simmer sauce about 5 minutes more or until liquid is reduced and slightly thickened.

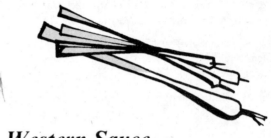

Western Sauce

This sauce can be kept for several weeks in the refrigerator. Spread it on beef; or you can try it on pork, poultry, and even fish if they're stronger-flavored ones.

  1 can (1 lb.) tomatoes
  2 cups water
  1 can (6 oz.) tomato paste
  2 dried chile peppers
  ½ cup tomato catsup
  2 tablespoons sugar
  2 teaspoons Worcestershire
  2 teaspoons chile powder
    Juice of 2 lemons
  ¼ cup wine vinegar
  2½ teaspoons salt
  ¼ teaspoon cayenne
  ¼ teaspoon liquid hot-pepper seasoning
  2 teaspoons freshly ground black pepper
  1 large onion, chopped
  1 clove garlic, chopped
  2 bay leaves
  ½ pound butter
  2 teaspoons dry mustard

Combine all ingredients and let simmer over low flame in covered pan for about 30 minutes. Strain through coarse sieve. Cool; pour into refrigerator containers and refrigerate until needed.

Fresh Red Chile Salsa

This easy version of Mexican red chile sauce is made with fresh tomatoes. Fish with assertive flavors, as well as beef, pork, and poultry benefit by this sauce.

Peel 4 firm medium-sized red tomatoes and chop fine. Mix with 1 can (4 oz.) drained, chopped green chile peppers, 1 medium-sized, finely chopped onion, ¼ teaspoon salt, and a dash pepper. Stir in 2 tablespoons cider vinegar and a dash liquid hot-pepper seasoning. Let stand for 1 to 2 hours before serving to allow flavors to blend well. Makes 4 to 5 cups.

Flavored Butters

You can use flavored butter to season your barbecued meat, vegetables, or to spread on French bread.

Flavored butters are not intended for long-time storage; for best flavor, plan to use them within a week or two. Butter and margarine can be used interchangeably in most of the recipes that follow.

Fines Herbes Butter. Combine ½ cup (¼ lb.) butter or margarine, 1 tablespoon minced parsley (fresh or freeze-dried), 1 tablespoon chopped chives (fresh or freeze-dried), ½ teaspoon tarragon, ½ teaspoon chervil, ¼ teaspoon salt, and dash of pepper; beat until fluffy. Cover and refrigerate.

Suggested use: Try on hamburger patties, liver, and green vegetables.

Garlic Butter. Combine ½ cup (¼ lb.) butter or margarine, 2 to 3 cloves garlic (minced or mashed), and 2 tablespoons minced parsley (fresh or freeze-dried); beat until fluffy. Cover and refrigerate.

Suggested use: Melt this on salmon or on lamb chops or beef steaks; brush on shish kebabs.

Basil Butter. Combine ½ cup (¼ lb.) butter or margarine, ½ cup lightly packed, chopped fresh basil leaves (or 2 tablespoons dried basil), 2 tablespoons minced parsley, 1 tablespoon lemon juice, and ¼ cup grated Parmesan cheese in blender and whirl until smooth (or crush basil and parsley with mortar and pestle, and beat together with other ingredients). Cover and refrigerate.

Suggested use: Season baked potatoes, zucchini, eggplant; melt on fish.

Red Onion Butter. Sauté 1 medium-sized red onion (finely chopped) in 2 tablespoons butter until soft, about 5 minutes; add 2 tablespoons dry red wine and cook until all liquid is evaporated. Cool thoroughly. Then combine the onion mixture, ½ cup (¼ lb.) butter, and ¼ teaspoon salt; whirl in the blender or beat until fluffy. Cover and refrigerate.

Suggested use: Season beef steak, ground beef, veal, or lamb chops.

Shallot Butter. Sauté 3 fresh shallots (peeled and minced) in 2 tablespoons butter until soft, about 5 minutes; add 2 tablespoons dry Sherry and cook until all the liquid is evaporated. Cool thoroughly, then combine with ½ cup (¼ lb.) butter and ¼ teaspoon salt. Beat until fluffy. Cover and refrigerate.

Suggested use: Serve on lamb, beef, or veal cuts; melt and use to baste chicken pieces when you barbecue them; season baked potatoes or other vegetables.

Maître d'Hôtel Butter. Combine ½ cup (¼ lb.) butter or margarine, 2 teaspoons lemon juice, 2 teaspoons minced parsley, ¼ teaspoon salt, ¼ teaspoon whole thyme, and ⅛ teaspoon pepper; beat until fluffy. Cover and refrigerate.

Suggested use: Melt and use as baste on chicken or fish while grilling.

Mustard Butter. Prepare Maître d'Hôtel Butter as directed above, omitting thyme. Beat in 2 tablespoons Dijon-style mustard.

Suggested use: Spread on hamburgers, steaks, liver, or fish.

Dill Butter. Press 2 hard-cooked egg yolks through a wire strainer; combine with ½ cup (¼ lb.) butter or margarine, 4½ teaspoons dill weed, ½ teaspoon salt, and ⅛ teaspoon white or black pepper; beat until fluffy. Cover and refrigerate.

Suggested use: Season shrimp, salmon, or other fish.

Tomato-Ginger Baste with Variations

Brush this tomato-ginger baste (or the cranberry or apricot variation) on chicken, pork chops, spareribs, or hamburgers.

1½ cups catsup
¼ cup soy sauce
⅓ cup brown sugar, firmly packed
1 teaspoon salt
1 teaspoon dry mustard
1 clove garlic, crushed
2½ teaspoons ground ginger

Combine catsup, soy sauce, brown sugar, salt, mustard, garlic, and ginger, mixing well. Cover and let stand 2 hours to blend flavors, or refrigerate until ready to use. Brush on meat during the last 10 minutes of cooking. (It will burn easily, so watch it carefully.)

Cranberry-Ginger Baste

Omit catsup and add 1 small can (7 oz.) jellied cranberry sauce and ¼ cup more brown sugar.

Smoky Apricot Baste

Omit catsup and soy sauce and add 1 cup puréed canned apricots, ¼ teaspoon liquid smoke flavoring, and 3 tablespoons lemon juice.

SIDE DISHES

When you barbecue an entrée for dinner, take advantage of the barbecue fire for cooking other foods on the menu. Many fruits and vegetables have a natural affinity for the smoky barbecue flavor and can be cooked directly on the grill. Others may be wrapped in foil and heated on the grill or near the coals, steaming in their own juices or in added butter or liquid.

Fruits and vegetables can also be cooked on skewers. Since they generally take a shorter cooking time than meat, it's best not to put them on the same skewers.

Zucchini-Tomato Kebabs
SKEWER-COOKED

Thread skewers with the vegetables either just before grilling or several hours in advance (refrigerate).

  2 medium-sized zucchini
    About 2 cups salted water
½ teaspoon oregano
    Cherry tomatoes
    Melted butter
  2 tablespoons Parmesan cheese
    Salt
    Pepper

Parboil zucchini for 4 to 5 minutes in salted water seasoned with oregano. Remove and cut each crosswise into 4 sections. Thread alternately with cherry tomatoes on 2 small skewers. Baste with melted butter and cook about 8 inches above hot coals for about 10 minutes, turning and basting frequently. Just before removing from grill, sprinkle each kebab with 1 tablespoon Parmesan cheese and a dash of salt and pepper. Serve immediately. Makes 2 servings.

Mixed Vegetable Grill
SKEWER-COOKED

Prepare the vegetables early in the day and let them marinate until you are ready to cook them; then skewer vegetables and cook over hot coals.

Plan to serve approximately 1 cup vegetables per person—or enough to fill a medium-length skewer. A good selection includes: frozen artichoke hearts (thawed), cucumber chunks or slices, eggplant cubes, small whole mushrooms, pieces of green pepper, and cherry tomatoes.

Cut vegetables in bite-sized pieces; marinate for several hours in your favorite French dressing, or in a mixture of 1 cup salad oil, ⅓ cup lemon juice, ¼ teaspoon salt, dash pepper, and dash sugar. Just before cooking, remove vegetables from marinade and string on skewers. Place skewers over coals; cook 3 to 5 minutes, turning once. Baste vegetables with some of the marinade while they are cooking.

Ginger-Buttered Fruit Kebabs
SKEWER-COOKED

Children can handle this last-minute job of grilling fruit kebabs. Transfer some hot coals from the barbecue to a small hibachi if space is short on the barbecue.

For each fruit kebab, cut a thick half-slice of orange with peel, a red apple wedge, a thick diagonal slice of banana, and a fresh pineapple chunk (or use canned pineapple chunks). Thread small bamboo skewers each with the 4 fruits; grill 5 to 10 minutes or until lightly browned, basting frequently with ginger butter (recipe follows). Allow 1 fruit kebab for each serving. Serve warm.

Ginger Butter

In a small pan, melt ½ cup (¼ lb.) butter; stir in 2 tablespoons sugar and 1 teaspoon ground ginger. Makes enough baste for 12 to 18 kebabs.

Mushrooms en Brochette, Flambé
SKEWER-COOKED

To dramatize a steak, serve it with mushrooms grilled on skewers and flamed.

2 pounds medium-sized, uniform mushrooms, cleaned (remove stems and save for another purpose)
Melted butter
Olive oil or salad oil
Salt
Pepper
¼ cup cognac, warmed

Using sharply pointed skewers, carefully impale mushroom caps on 6 skewers. Brush them all over with a mixture of half melted butter and half olive oil or salad oil; sprinkle with salt and pepper. Grill over charcoal turning to brown on all sides, and basting once or twice with the olive oil and butter mixture. Cooking time is about 10 minutes. Arrange mushrooms on a hot flameproof dish and pour over them the warmed Cognac; light. When flames die down, serve with steak. Makes 6 servings.

Pineapple-Banana-Bacon Grill
SKEWER-COOKED

Bacon flavor permeates the chunks of fruit as you grill the fruit on skewers.

About 12 strips thickly sliced bacon
1 small pineapple, cubed
3 large bananas, sliced 1-inch thick

Use wooden skewers for these. For each skewer, weave 1 strip bacon around 3 cubes of fresh pineapple and 2 banana slices. Keep foods chilled until time to cook. Grill over hot coals until bacon is cooked (about 2 minutes), turning as needed. Makes 6 servings.

Spit-Roasted Fruits and Vegetables
SPIT-ROASTED

Fruits and vegetables take longer to cook by this method than by roasting in the coals, but the slow steady turning causes them to cook more evenly. Whole green peppers, acorn squash, zucchini, potatoes, onions, yams, apples, and eggplant can all be prepared in this manner. If you choose fruits and vegetables of uniform size, they will finish cooking at the same time. They will probably need less time than thick chunks of meat, however.

Before starting to cook them, brush vegetables with olive oil. The baste or marinade which you use on the meat can also be used to baste the fruit and vegetables. Remove them from the fire when they stop turning with the spit (interior is cooked at this point).

Ideas for Grilling Vegetables
GRILL-COOKED

· Use cooked artichoke bottoms; marinate them in French dressing before grilling.
· Cook unpeeled carrots just until tender; peel and dip in butter; then heat on grill.
· Cut green peppers in quarters; remove seeds and dip in olive oil before grilling.

Tangy Eggplant Wedges
GRILL-COOKED

If you're barbecuing lamb or beef, you can cook eggplant at the same time to serve with the meat.

½ cup olive oil or salad oil
2 tablespoons white wine vinegar
1 clove garlic, mashed
2 teaspoons salt
¼ teaspoon oregano
1 medium-sized eggplant, washed, stem removed (do not peel)

Mix and shake together olive or salad oil, vinegar, garlic, salt, and oregano. Let stand for 1 hour or more to blend flavors. Shake well just before using. Cut eggplant lengthwise into 8 equal-sized wedges. Brush with oil mixture on all sides and place on grill over hot coals. Cook until tender, turning once. Brush frequently with remaining oil mixture. Makes 4 servings.

Ideas for Grilling Fruits
GRILL-COOKED

· Cut unpeeled apples in thick slices and dip in butter. Grill on both sides, sprinkling with cinnamon and sugar toward the end of the cooking.

· Remove pits from dates and stuff with Cheddar cheese; wrap in bacon and grill for an appetizer.

· Wrap fresh figs in bacon and grill them until bacon is crisp.

· Cut unpeeled oranges in thick slices; dip in melted butter and dust lightly with flour. Heat on both sides.

· Peel bananas and cut in half. Wrap with bacon and grill on both sides. Or use unpeeled bananas and make a slit about 3 inches long in the skin of each one. Force 1 tablespoon of honey into each opening and let stand for ½ hour. Place on grill and cook for about 8 minutes, turning frequently.

· Cut a fresh pineapple into 8 lengthwise spears. Place in baking pan and drip honey — about a tablespoon to a section — over the fruit. Let stand for ½ hour and then grill. Or, use sliced pineapple, either canned or fresh, and brush with melted butter before broiling on both sides.

· Cut grapefruit in halves and remove seeds. Loosen segments from the skin and section membranes. Cover with brown or granulated sugar. Dot tops with butter; pour about a tablespoon of Sherry or rum over each half. Place on grill and cook until fruit is thoroughly heated.

· Use fresh or canned peaches. If fresh, they should be peeled and halved. Brush with butter and grill, cut side down, until brown; then turn and fill cavities with butter and brown sugar, and continue grilling until brown on the bottom. If desired, put a little Sherry or rum in the cavities and serve them as a dessert with cold sour cream or ice cream.

Parboiled Vegetables en Skewer
SKEWER-COOKED

These skewers simplify the vegetable accompaniment for barbecued meat; you can use the same basting sauce for the vegetables as for the meat.

Parboil zucchini (cut in 1-inch lengths), mushrooms, and small white onions for 3 minutes in boiling water and string on skewers. Grill over coals for 5 minutes. Brush with melted butter or the baste being used on barbecued meat.

Soy-Pineapple Apple Slices
GRILL-COOKED

The same sauce used for basting these apple slices can be used to baste chicken.

Core apples and cut into slices about ⅜ inch thick. Place on barbecue grill and broil until tender (about 5 minutes on each side), basting with mixture of ¾ cup soy sauce, ¾ cup unsweetened pineapple juice, and 3 tablespoons sugar.

Charcoal-Roasted Corn on the Cob
GRILL-COOKED

There are many ways to cook corn on the cob over a charcoal fire, and these are just a few of the variations:

1) Use unhusked ears. Lay back husks and remove silk. Return husks to former positions and wire them into place (with any fine wire) at center and near tip of cob, covering the kernels as well as possible. Roast on the grill 15 or 20 minutes, turning 3 or 4 times so that all surfaces are exposed to the heat. Snip the wires with wire cutter; husk the ears (gloves are necessary) and serve.

2) Open husk at one end; let about 2 tablespoons of barbecue sauce run inside the ear. Smooth husk back in place; tie and cook as above.

Buttered Tomatoes
GRILL-COOKED

Cut firm tomatoes in halves, brush with butter, sprinkle with salt and pepper, and grill, cut side down. When brown, turn, brush with more butter, and continue cooking until barely tender. Buttered toast crumbs may be sprinkled on the cut side after turning.

3) Pull husks back, remove silk, brush corn generously with garlic butter. Replace husks and place ears on grill. Dip a clean burlap sack in warm water, wring it out slightly, and place it over the ears so that they will steam. Let the ears grill 10 minutes on one side. Remove burlap, turn ears, re-cover with burlap, sprinkle it with more water. Grill 5 or 10 minutes longer.

4) Strip ears down to last 3 or 4 husks and place in ice water 30 minutes or longer. Drain well and grill for only 15 or 20 minutes.

5) Husk corn, wrap in bacon, and grill until bacon is crisp and the exposed corn brown.

6) Husk and remove silk from each ear of corn. Place each ear on a sheet of heavy foil. Mix together ½ cup melted butter and 3 tablespoons soy sauce; pour about 1 tablespoon of the mixture over each of 12 ears of corn. Wrap securely, using a freezer-style wrap. To cook, place in the barbecue coals for 15 minutes, turning several times.

Roasted Stuffed Eggplant
COAL-COOKED

When barbecuing for a crowd of hungry people, stuff eggplants and roast them in the coals beneath the meat.

6 large eggplants, halved lengthwise
6 large onions, chopped
1 cup minced parsley
1 cup (½ lb.) butter or margarine
  Salt
  Pepper
  Juice of 2 or 3 lemons

Scoop out centers of eggplants, leaving about ½-inch walls. Dice centers, combine with onions and parsley; simmer this mixture in butter or margarine until vegetables are tender. Season to taste with salt and pepper and lemon juice. Spoon mixture into eggplant shells and put shells back together. Seal each in 2 layers of heavy foil. Roast on hot coals for 30 minutes, or until vegetable feels soft. Turn occasionally; do not pierce foil. Cut in quarters. Makes 24 servings.

Mushroom Caps in Butter
GRILL-COOKED

Select large mushrooms; allow 2 or 3 for each serving. Cut stems flush with caps. Dip in melted butter (seasoned with tarragon, chives, or dill, if desired) and place in a hinged wire broiler, cap sides up. Cook, cap sides up, over hot coals; do not spill juices that accumulate in the mushrooms. Season with salt and pepper. Serve as an appetizer or with any meat, shellfish, or poultry.

Grilling in Foil
GRILL-COOKED

Wrapping vegetables or fruits in foil before grilling them eliminates the smoky flavor, and makes the food easy to serve and eat. The following ideas are easy to do.

Vegetables. Some vegetables to wrap in foil and cook on the grill are as follows: shredded peeled beets, sliced carrots, corn cut from the cob, sliced peeled eggplant, sliced mushrooms, sliced onions, sliced green peppers, sliced or diced white or sweet potatoes, shelled peas, and sliced squash.

Season vegetables with salt and pepper and plenty of butter before wrapping. If desired, vegetables may also be cooked in combinations, such as onions and potatoes, corn and green peppers, peas and mushrooms.

Fruits. Here are suggestions for fruits which may be heated in a foil wrapping on the barbecue; serve them with grilled meats or as a dessert for a barbecued meal:
· Apples. Peel and slice; season with butter and sugar, then with cinnamon, coriander, or mace. Wrap in foil and grill until fork tender.
· Bananas. Peel and slice or quarter; season with sugar and butter; wrap in foil and grill.
· Oranges. Peel and divide into segments. Season with butter, sugar, and cinnamon or rosemary. Wrap and grill.
· Peaches. Peel and cut in slices. Season with butter and brown sugar. Wrap and grill.
· Pears. Peel and slice; season with butter, sugar, and ginger, or add slivered candied ginger. Wrap and grill.
· Pineapple. Use pineapple chunks. Season with butter and sugar. Wrap and grill.

Cooking in the Coals
COAL-COOKED

To cook fruits or vegetables right in the coals, first wrap them securely in a double layer of foil; then place in or around the ashes. Turn once or twice during the cooking. Test for doneness by piercing through the foil with a long-pronged fork.

Apples. Core apples and fill holes with sugar and a piece of butter; you can also add cinnamon or nutmeg, if you wish. Wrap in foil and cook for 30 minutes, or until fork tender.

Bananas. Wrap unpeeled bananas in foil and roast like apples; or peel the bananas, dip in melted butter, and sprinkle with sugar before wrapping.

Beets. Wrap whole unpeeled beets in foil and roast until tender. Serve with butter and lemon wedges. Let guests peel and season their own beets, or if you prefer, you can peel the beets before roasting.

Potatoes. Wrap unpeeled potatoes in foil and roast until fork tender, or if you like a hard, blackened skin (and many do), roast potatoes without wrapping. Cook until fork tender and turn during cooking. They will take from 30 to 60 minutes. Serve with plenty of butter or with sour cream and chives. Sweet potatoes or yams may be cooked the same way.

Eggplant. Wrap a whole eggplant in foil and roast it over the coals. When fork tender, the skin will peel off easily.

Onions. Wrap whole peeled or unpeeled onions in foil and roast until fork tender. Serve with butter.

Classic Barbecue Accompaniments

The pièce de résistance of your barbecue will, of course, be the meat that you lift piping hot from the grill, the spit, or the coals. The side dishes that you serve with this flavorsome main course should not in any way detract from it; yet they should be sufficient to satisfy the hearty appetites that go with outdoor dining. The classic favorites are surprisingly simple:

- A cool crisp salad, deftly seasoned and skillfully tossed.
- Hot-buttered French bread, with or without garlic.
- Relishes for flavor contrast — all kinds of pickles and olives, green onions, radishes, celery, carrots, tomatoes, green pepper, raw cauliflower, cucumbers.
- A wine of your choosing.
- Gallons of coffee or tea, iced or hot.
- For dessert, a tempting cheese tray, chilled ripe fruit (melon, papaya, pineapple, strawberries), ice cream, berry pie, or a big cake.

Onion Packets
COAL-COOKED

Onions, seasoned and wrapped in foil, can be cooked right in the hot barbecue coals.

For each serving, peel 2 small white onions and make a cross in the stem end. Place on a small sheet of heavy foil, dot with butter, and season with salt and pepper. Wrap securely. To cook, place directly in the barbecue coals for 30 minutes.

Foil-Barbecued Potatoes
GRILL-COOKED

Foil-potatoes cook quickly on the barbecue when you start with the vegetable partially cooked.

Use leftover cooked whole potatoes, or precook fresh potatoes until almost tender. Peel and cut each into 4 sections. Place thin onion slices between potato sections and reassemble potatoes. Place each potato on a square of heavy duty foil, the center of which is spread with 1 tablespoon butter or margarine. Wrap foil tightly to enclose potato and hold sections together. Barbecue for 20 to 30 minutes, or until onion is tender.

Grilled Cheese Appetizer
GRILL-COOKED

Grill this cheese over *very slow* coals—if your fire is too hot, the cheese will burn on the bottom and boil over. When cheese has completely melted, remove from fire; return to heat occasionally to keep warm and melted as it is served.

1 to 1¼ pounds jack cheese,
    cut in ¼-inch-thick slices
3 medium-sized tomatoes
    About ¼ cup diced canned California
    green chiles
3 tablespoons minced onion
½ teaspoon salt
    About 2 minced chiles jalapeños
    (or other hot chiles)
    About 1 dozen frozen or fresh corn tortillas

Place a single layer of cheese slices in an 8-inch pottery or heatproof dish or cake or pie pan to ½ to ¾-inch depth. Cover and set aside. To make the tomato and green chile sauce, peel and finely chop the tomatoes. Mix with the canned California green chiles, onion, salt, and chiles jalapeños. Heat tortillas by placing on a medium-hot griddle or in a heavy frying pan over medium-high heat; heat about 30 seconds on a side, or until soft. Stack tortillas and cut in quarters. Wrap in a tea towel and keep warm until you are ready to serve.

Place plate of cheese over very slow coals to melt. Have your guests make their own appetizers by spreading some of the softened cheese on a tortilla wedge, spooning on a little of the hot sauce, then folding tortillas to enclose filling. Makes about 48 appetizers.

Three Snacks Over the Coals
SKEWER-COOKED

Toasting a snack over the fireplace flames or campfire is always fun, especially for children. Here are three ideas to add variety to fireside refreshments.

Ham-Broiled Holiday Cherries. Cut boiled ham into strips about ½ inch wide. Wrap around red or green glacéed cherries; spear onto long skewers and broil over flame until ham is crisply browned.

Frank and Cheese Roll-Ups. Trim crusts from an unsliced sandwich loaf of bread; cut into thin slices, lengthwise. Spread with a creamy cheese spread made as follows: Combine 1 small package (3 oz.) cream cheese with 1 teaspoon chicken stock base (or 1 bouillon cube) dissolved in 2 teaspoons warm water, and 1 tablespoon pickle relish.

Plump up cocktail frankfurters by letting them stand in hot water for 5 minutes; then dry (or use canned cocktail frankfurters, thoroughly drained). Arrange, lengthwise, at edge of bread slice. Roll up and wrap in waxed paper or foil; refrigerate for several hours. Slice between frankfurters; spear with skewers and toast.

Toasted Bacon and Bread Poles. Cut unsliced, ready-to-bake French bread into poles about 1 inch across and 4 or 5 inches long. Spiral strips of bacon around each pole, securing the ends with toothpicks. Cook on grill over hot coals.

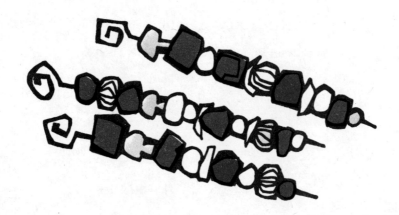

INDEX

A

Accessories for
  Barbecues, 8
Accompaniments
  Classic Barbecue, 90
  for skewers, 24
Albacore
  How to Grill, 75
  Soy-Grilled Steaks, 73
Anchovy
  Butter, 36
  Shrimp Appetizers, 79
Appetizers
  Beef Jerky, 43
  Beef-Oyster, 21
  Butterflied Shrimp, 75
  Chinese Pork, 21
  Grilled Cheese, 91
  Hawaiian Beef, 26
  Indonesian Chicken, 62
  Lamb Sosaties with
    Fruit, 46
  Shrimp and Anchovy, 79
  Spicy Shrimp, 79
  Three Snacks over the
    Coals, 91
Apples
  Cinnamon, 61
  Cooking in the
    Coals, 90
  Soy Marinade for
    Pork, 51
Apricot, Smoky Baste,
  83, 85
Aromatic Additives, 14
Artichoke, Top Round
  Steak, 41
Avocado
  Cheeseburgers with
    Guacamole, 36
  Guacamole, 27

B

Balance Weights, 9
Bananas
  Cooking in the
    Coals, 90
  Pineapple-Bacon
    Grill, 87
Barbecue Accessories, 8
  Balance Weights for
    Spit, 9
  Brushes for Basting, 8
  Forks, 8
  Knives, 9
  Mitts, 8
  Pliers, 9
  Skewers, 9
  Spatulas, 8

Barbecue Accessories
  (cont'd.)
  Spit Forks, 9
  Thermometers, 8
  Tongs, 8
Barbecues
  Braziers, 6
  Ceramic, 6
  Covered, 6
  Dampers, 7
  Electric, 7
  Foil Cover, 14
  Gas, 7
  Gas Fuel, 7
  Kamado, 7
  Small, portable, 6
  Wagon, 7
Barracuda
  How to Grill, 75
  Steaks, 75
Basque, Barbecued
  Lamb, 48
Bastes
  Basic Chicken, 63
  Basic Lemon Butter, 83
  Brandy, 64
  Brown Sugar-Tarragon
    Vinegar, 63
  Coffee, 49
  Cranberry-Ginger, 85
  French Dressing, 63
  Golden Glaze, 63
  Golden Papaya, 80
  Herb, 45, 63
  Herb Butter for
    Chicken or
    Turkey, 83
  Lemon-Herb Butter, 63
  Lime Sauce, 48
  Mustard-Honey, 63
  Parsley Orange for
    Lamb, 83
  Purple Plum, 80
  Savory for
    Hamburgers, 83
  Savory Raisin, 81
  Smoky Apricot, 85
  Smoky Peach or
    Apricot, 83
  Soy-Ginger
    Marinade, 82
  Spiced Currant, 63
  Sweet-Sour
    Pineapple, 82
  Teriyaki, 63
  Tomato-Ginger with
    Variations, 85
Beef
  Barbecued
    Hanging
      Tenderlion, 35
    Kidneys, 56
    Rib Bones, 38
    Stroganoff, 33
  Brains, Butter-
    Broiled, 58
  Chef's Chuck Roast, 35

Beef (cont'd.)
  Chuck Steak with
    Anchovy Butter, 36
  Cumin Steak Strips
    and Cheese, 40
  Family Round Steak, 31
  Filet Mignon
    Aubergine, 28
  Garlic Steak in a
    Crust, 34
  Giant Lobster
    Kebabs, 25
  Ginger Teriyaki, 27
  Grilled Eye of Round
    Steaks, 33
  Hawaiian Beef
    Appetizers, 26
  Heart
    Peruvian
      Anticuchos, 57
    Thick-Sliced, 59
  Herbed Shanks with
    Summer Squash, 40
  Honolulu Steak, 28
  Japanese-Style
    Steak, 34
  Jerky, 43
  Lazy Holiday Roast, 42
  Korean Shortrib
    Barbecue, 41
  Liver
    Foie de Veau en
      Brochette, 56
    Marinated Steak, 58
    Mi'Laaf Mashivi, 56
    n' Bacon Grill, 57
    Superb, 57
    Whole with Salt
      Pork, 59
  Marinated Shortribs, 38
  Oyster Appetizer, 21
  Oyster-Stuffed Market
    Steaks, 31
  Oyster-Topped Fillet, 41
  Pakistani Kebabs, 24
  Pizza-Style Cube
    Steaks, 36
  Porterhouse with
    Bèarnaise, 32
  Rib Eye Steaks, 28
  Rosemary Barbecued
    Sirloin, 39
  Savory Chuck Roast, 43
  Sirloin à la
    Mirabeau, 31
  Skirt Steak with
    Burgundy Sauce, 34
  Skirt Steaks
    Teriyaki, 35
  Skirts-Kebab, 21
  Smoked Sirloin Tip, 42
  Steak
    au Poivre, 29
    Kebabs, 29
    Jalisco, 32
    on the Coals, 40

Beef (cont'd.)
  Sandwiches with
    Mushroom Sauce, 30
  with Roquefort
    Butter, 33
  Sweetbreads and Steak
    Brochette, 22
  Teriyaki Steak
    Strips, 35
  Tenderloin Steak
    Casanova, 28
  Tongue
    Broiled, 59
    Hickory-Smoked, 59
  Top Round Steak with
    Artichoke Hearts, 41
  Tournedos Héloïse, 30
  Western Barbecue
    Steak, 32
  Whole Fillet with Blue-
    Cheese Log, 29
Beef, Ground
  Beef and Cheese
    Stacks, 37
  Chef's, 39
  Cheeseburgers with
    Guacamole, 36
  Crunchy Onion-Beef
    Burgers, 36
  Hamburger Steak in
    the Round, 37
  Individual Meat and
    Spinach Loaves, 58
  Mushroom-Filled
    Hamburger Cups, 39
  Pizza-Flavored Meat
    Loaf, 42
  Shish Koftesi, 22
  Soy-Dipped
    Hamburgers, 38
  Stretched
    Hamburger, 37
Beef, Sauces, etc.
  Bercy Butter for
    Grilled Meats, 82
  Cheddar-Sherry
    Sauce, 81
  Fresh Red Chile
    Salsa, 84
  Fresh Tomato and
    Green Chile, 27
  Fresh Tomato
    Barbecue, 84
  Guacamole, 27
  Mexican Sauces, 27
  Red Wine Marinade, 81
  Red Chile Sauce, 27
  Savory Baste, 83
  Savory Raisin Baste, 81
  Shallot Sauce, 26
  Soy-Ginger Marinade
    and Baste, 82
  Soy Lemon
    Marinade, 27
  Sweet-Sour Tomato
    Barbecue Sauce, 84

Beef Sauces (cont'd.)
Three-Way Tomato
Relish, 82
Tomato-Ginger Baste
with Variations, 85
Western Sauce, 84
Beets, Cooking in the
Coals, 90
Buffalo, in Tomato-Wine
Sauce, 60
Butters
Anchovy, 36
Basil, 85
Bercy for Grilled
Meats, 82
Dill, 85
Fines Herbes, 85
Garlic, 85
Ghee, 49
Ginger, 86
Green Chile, 60
Herb, 66
Mâitre d' Hôtel, 85
Mustard, 85
Red Onion, 85
Roquefort, 33
Sesame-Cheese, 61
Shallot, 85
Tarragon, 22
Vegetable, 61

C

Cantaloupe
Ham Steak, 51
Roast Pork Loin on
Melon Ring, 55
Cheese
Beef and Cheese
Stacks, 37
Blue Log, 29
Cheddar-Sherry
Sauce, 81
Cheeseburgers with
Guacamole, 36
Frank and Cheese
Roll-ups, 91
Muenster, Cumin
Steak Strips, 40
Steak with Roquefort
Butter, 33
Chinese
Pork Appetizers, 20
Ribs, 54
Surprised Squab, 69
Chicken
Barbecued Breasts, 65
Barbecued Spanish
Style, 64
Grilled, 63
Herbed, 63
Indonesian
Appetizers, 62
Lemon-Basted with
Peaches, 65
Liver Kebabs, 25
Orange-Baked, 65

Chicken (cont'd.)
Pakistani
Barbecued, 65
Kebabs, 24
Ranch-Style, 66
Smoke-Glazed, 64
Smoked with Brandy
Baste, 64
Spicy Yogurt, 62
Spit-Roasted, 66
Spread Eagle, 63
Chicken, Sauces, etc.
Herb Butter Baste, 83
Golden Papaya
Baste, 80
Purple Plum Baste, 80
Smoky Peach or Apricot
Baste, 83
Soy-Ginger Marinade
and Baste, 82
Sweet-Sour Pineapple
Baste, 82
Sweet-Sour Tomato
Barbecue Sauce, 84
Tomato-Ginger Baste
with Variations, 85
Coal-Cooked
Apples, 90
Bananas, 90
Beef, Steak on the
Coals, 40
Beets, 90
Eggplant, 90
Fish, Smoked in
Paper, 76
Onions, 90
Onion Packets, 90
Potatoes, 90
Poultry
Orange-Baked
Chicken, 65
Roasted Stuffed
Eggplant, 89
Corn, Charcoal-Roasted
on the Cob, 88

D

Duck
Broiled Mallard, 71
Wild, Spit-Roasted, 70
Duckling
Kamo No Koma-Giri, 70
How to Cook, 69
Orange Barbecued, 69
with Orange Baste, 68
with Raisin Sauce, 70

E

East Indian
Satés, 23
Spicy Yogurt
Chicken, 62
Eggplant
Cooking in the
Coals, 90

Eggplant (cont'd.)
Lamb Chops a la
Castellane, 47
Roasted Stuffed, 89
Tangy Wedges, 87

F

Fire Starters
Electric, 10
Chimney, 10
Inflammable Liquids
and Jellies, 10
Firebed
Liners, 9
Preparation, 9
Firemanship, Arranging
the Coals, 10
Firepit Cooking, 15
Beans, 18
Beef, 18
Coals, 18
Covering the Pit, 18
Fire, 18
Kind of Wood, 18
Meat Preparation, 18
Pit, 18
Timing, 18
Fish
How to Grill, 75
Kebabs Piraeus, 78
Smoked in Paper, 76
Steaks with Bran, 77
White
Barbecued Lean, 73
Orange-Soy, 79
Slow-Smoked
Garlic, 78
with Fennel, 77
Fish and Shellfish,
see also Barracuda,
Salmon, Shrimp, etc.
Fish, Sauces, etc.
Basic Lemon Butter
Baste, 83
Fresh Red Chile
Salsa, 84
Fresh Tomato Barbecue
Sauce, 84
Soy-Ginger Marinade
and Baste, 82
Sweet-Sour Pineapple
Baste, 82
Three-Way Tomato
Relish, 82
Western Sauce, 84
Flounder, Smoked in
Paper, 76
Foil Hood for
Barbecues, 14
French
Brochette de Rognons
d' Agneau, 56
Dressing Baste, 63
Foie de Veau en
Brochette, 56

French (cont'd.)
Sweetbreads and Steak
Brochette, 22
Fruit, see also Apple,
Banana, Pineapple,
etc.
Cooking in the Coals, 90
Grilling in Foil, 89
Ideas for Grilling, 88
Skewer
Combinations, 24
Spit-Roasted, 87
Stuffing, 67
Fuel
Charcoal Briquets, 9
Coal, 9
Gas Barbecues, 7
Hardwood, 9

G

Game, see Buffalo,
Venison
Garlic
Butter, 85
Leg of Lamb with
Coffee Baste, 49
Slow-Smoked Fish, 78
Spareribs, 54
Steak in a Crust, 34
Ginger
Barbecued
Spareribs, 52
Beef Teriyaki, 27
Butter, 86
Buttered Fruit
Kebabs, 86
Glazes
Curry Honey, 23
Honey, 55
Goose, Crisp-Roasted, 71
Greek
Arni Souvlakia, 20
Fish Kebabs Piraeus, 78
Grill-Cooked
Beef
Barbecued Beef
Stroganoff, 33
Barbecued Hanging
Tenderloin, 35
Barbecued Rib
Bones, 38
Beefsteak Jalisco, 32
Chef's Chuck
Roast, 35
Chuck Steak with
Anchovy Butter, 36
Family Round Steak
Barbecue, 31
Filet Mignon
Aubergine, 28
Garlic Steak in a
Crust, 34
Ginger-Barbecued
Spareribs, 52
Grilled Eye of Round
Steaks, 33

Beef (cont'd.)
Herbed Beef
Shanks, 40
Honolulu Steak, 28
How to Make Beef
Jerky, 43
Japanese-Style
Steak, 34
Korean Shortrib
Barbecue, 41
Marinated Beef
Shortribs, 38
Oyster-Stuffed
Market Steaks, 31
Pizza-Style Cube
Steaks, 36
Porterhouse with
Béarnaise, 32
Rib Eye Steaks, 28
Savory Chuck
Roast, 43
Sirloin à la
Mirabeau, 31
Skirt Steak, 34
Skirt Steaks
Teriyaki, 35
Steak au Poivre, 29
Steak Sandwiches, 30
Steak with Roquefort
Butter, 33
Tenderloin Steak
Casanova, 28
Teriyaki Steak
Strips, 35
Tournedos Héloïse, 30
Western Barbecue
Steak, 32
Whole Fillet, 29
Beef, Ground
Beef and Cheese
Stacks, 37
Cheeseburgers with
Guacamole, 36
Chef's Ground
Beef, 39
Crunchy Onion-Beef
Burgers, 36
Hamburger Steak in
the Round, 37
Mushroom-Filled
Hamburger Cups, 39
Pizza-Flavored Meat
Loaf, 42
Soy-Dipped
Hamburgers, 38
Stretched
Hamburger, 37
Buttered Tomatoes, 88
Charcoal-Roasted Corn
on the Cob, 88

Fish and Shellfish
Barbecued Lean White
Fish, 73
Barracuda Steaks, 75
Boned Mackerel in
Crumb Crust, 73
Butterflied Trout, 77

Fish and Shellfish
(cont'd.)
Fish with Fennel, 77
How to Cook
Shellfish, 76
How to Grill Fish, 75
Orange-Soy Fish, 79
Slow-Smoked Garlic
Fish, 78
Soy-Grilled Albacore
Steaks, 73
Foil-Barbecued
Potatoes, 90
Game
Buffalo in Tomato-
Wine Sauce, 60
Grilled Venison
Steak, 60
Venison Steak with
Trio of Butters, 60
Grilled Cheese
Appetizers, 91
Grilling in Foil, 89
Ideas for Grilling
Fruits, 88
Ideas for Grilling
Vegetables, 87
Lamb
Breast or Shanks, 46
Butterflied Leg of
Lamb, 45, 46
Chelo Kebab, 47
Chops, 47
Leg Chops, 44
Lela ka Kabab, 49
Mushroom Caps in
Butter, 89
Pork
Barbecued Bacon with
Pineapple, 54
Crumb-Coated Pigs'
Feet, 52
Ginger-Barbecued
Spareribs, 52
Ham Steak with
Cantaloupe, 51
Pineapple
Spareribs, 53
Smoky Ham
Steaks, 51
Spicy Ham Steak, 52
Venezuelan Barbecued
Pork, 50
Poultry
Barbecued Breast of
Chicken, 65
Barbecued Chicken,
Spanish Style, 64
Broiled Mallard
Duck, 71
Grilled Chicken, 63
Herbed Chicken, 63
Lemon-Basted
Chicken, 65
Orange Barbecued
Duckling, 69
Pakistani Barbecued
Chicken, 65

Poultry (cont'd.)
Pheasant
Barbecue, 70
Ranch-Style
Chicken, 66
Spicy Yogurt
Chicken, 62
Spread Eagle
Chicken, 63
Soy-Pineapple Apple
Slices, 88
Tangy Eggplant
Wedges, 87
Variety Meats
Barbecued
Bologna, 59
Barbecued
Kidneys, 57
Barbecued
Sausages, 58
Buttered-Broiled
Brains, 58
Individual Meat and
Spinach Loaves, 58
Liver Superb, 57
Marinated Liver
Steak, 58
Thick-Sliced Beef
Heart, 59
Tripe Strips in
Butter, 56

Grill Cooking, 10
Arranging the
Firebed, 11
Charts, 12, 13
in Foil, 89
Temperature, 12, 13
Times, 12, 13

H

Halibut
Baluk Shish Kebab, 77
How to Grill, 75
Hamburger, see Beef,
Ground
Hawaiian
Beef Appetizers, 26
Honolulu Steaks, 28
Rolled Leg of Pork, 51
Herb
Baste, 45, 63
Butter, 66
Butter Baste for
Chicken or
Turkey, 83
Mayonnaise Sauce, 74
Wine Marinade, 81
Hollandaise
Sauces, 74
with Cucumber, 74
with Shrimp, 74
Hickory-Smoked
Ham for a Crowd, 53
Tongue, 59

Honey
Glazed Ham, 55
Wine Marinade for
Lamb, 81
Glaze, 55

I

Indian, Lela ka Kabab, 49
Indonesian
Chicken Appetizers, 62
Satés, 23
Iranian
Chelo Kebab, 47
Kebab Barg, 45
Italian
Lamb Chops a la
Castellane, 47
Pizza-Flavored Meat
Loaf, 42

J

Japanese
Kamo No Koma-
Giri, 70
Onigari Yaki, 78
Steak, 34
Jerky, Beef, 43

K

Kebab
Barg, 45
Sauce, 22

L

Lamb
Arni Souvlakia, 20
Barbecued Kidneys, 56
Basque-Barbecued, 48
Breast or Shanks, 46
Brochette de Rognons
d'Agneau 56
Butter-Broiled
Brains, 58
Butterflied Leg with
Herb Baste, 45
Butterflied Leg with
Mushrooms, 46
Chelo Kebab, 47
Chops a la
Castellane, 47
Cubes, 21
Garlic Leg of Lamb, 49
Easy Leg, 48
Ground, 22
in Onion Juice, 21
Kebab Barg, 45
Leg Chops, 44
Lela ka Kabab, 49
Lime-Basted Leg, 48
Liver Superb, 57
Liver with Salt
Pork, 59

Lamb (cont'd.)
Pakistani Kebabs, 24
Rolls with Curry Honey
Glaze, 23
Russian Shashlik, 44
Sosaties with Fruit, 46
Smoked Leg, 48
Lamb, Sauces, etc.
Basic Sauces, 45
Bercy Butter for Grilled
Meats, 82
Cheddar-Sherry
Sauce, 81
Honey Wine
Marinade, 81
Parsley Orange
Baste, 83
Smoky Peach or
Apricot Baste, 83
Lebanese, Mi'Laaf
Mashivi, 56
Lemon
Basted Chicken with
Peaches, 65
Butter Sauce, 39
Herb Butter Baste, 63
Rice Stuffing, 72
Lobster
Giant Beef Kebabs, 25
How to Clean, 76
How to Cook, 76

M

Mackerel, Boned in
Crumb Crust, 73
Marinades
Apple-Soy for Pork, 51
Herb Wine, 81
Honey Wine, 81
Red Wine, 30, 81
Soy-Ginger, 82
Soy Lemon for Beef, 27
Teriyaki, 33
Mayonnaise
Brown Butter Almond
Sauce, 74
Herb Sauce, 74
Horseradish Sauce, 74
Mexican
Beefsteak Jalisco, 32
Cheeseburgers with
Guacamole, 36
Sauces for Beef, 27
Mushrooms
Butterflied Leg of
Lamb, 46
Caps in Butter, 89
en Brochette,
Flambé, 87
Filled Hamburger
Cups, 39
Sautéed, 39
Mustard
Butter, 85
Honey Baste, 63

O

Onion
Cooking in the Coals, 90
Packets, 90
Orange
Barbecued Duckling, 69
Baste, 68
Baked Chicken, 65
Celery Stuffing, 69
Gravy, 69
Soy Fish, 79
Oyster
Beef Appetizers, 21
Shellfish Kebabs, 78
Stuffed Market
Steaks, 31
Stuffing, 31
Topped Beef Fillet, 41

P

Pakistani
Barbecued Chicken, 65
Kebabs, 24
Peach
Lemon-Basted
Chicken, 65
Smoky Baste, 83
Pepper Steak, 29
Peruvian Anticuchos, 57
Pheasant
Barbecue, 70
with Cashew
Stuffing, 71
Pineapple
Banana-Bacon Grill, 87
Barbecued Bacon, 54
Soy Apple Slices, 88
Spareribs, 53
Pork
Barbecued Bacon with
Pineapple, 54
Barbecued Kidneys, 56
Chinese Appetizers, 21
Chinese Ribs, 54
Crumb-Coated Pigs'
Feet, 52
Garlic Spareribs, 54
Ginger-Barbecued
Spareribs, 52
Ground, Individual Meat
and Spinach
Loaves, 58
Ham Steak with
Cantaloupe, 51
Hickory-Smoked Ham
for a Crowd, 53
Honey-Glazed Ham, 55
Indonesian Satés, 23
Liver 'n Bacon Grill, 57
Loin with Prunes, 52
Pineapple Spareribs, 53
Roast Loin on Melon
Ring, 55
Rolled Leg, Hawaiian-
Style, 51

Pork (cont'd.)
Satés Bali, 50
Smoked Ribs in
Barbecue Sauce, 54
Smoky Ham Steaks, 51
Spicy Ham Steak, 52
Spit-Roasted Suckling
Pig, 53
Venezuelan
Barbecued, 50
Whole Liver with Salt
Pork, 59
Pork, Sauces, etc.
Fresh Red Chili
Salsa, 84
Fresh Tomato Barbecue
Sauce, 84
Golden Papaya Baste, 80
Purple Plum Baste, 80
Red Wine Marinade, 81
Smoky Peach or Apricot
Baste, 83
Soy-Ginger Marinade
and Baste, 82
Sweet-Sour Pineapple
Baste, 82
Sweet-Sour Tomato
Barbecue Sauce, 84
Three-Way Tomato
Relish, 82
Tomato-Ginger Baste
with Variations, 85
Western Sauce, 84
Potatoes
Cooking in the Coals, 90
Foil-Barbecued, 90
Poultry, see Chicken,
Duck, Turkey, etc.

R

Raisin
Duckling with
Sauce, 70
Savory Baste, 81
Rice
Chello, 45
Salmon with Lemon
Stuffing, 72
with Sausage, 64
Rockfish, Smoked in
Paper, 76
Russian Shashlik, 44

S

Salmon
Baluk Shish Kebab, 77
How to Grill, 75
Smoked Fresh
Fillet, 73
Smoked in Paper, 76
with Lemon Rice
Stuffing, 72
Sauces
All-Purpose
Barbecue, 83

Sauces (cont'd.)
Basting for Lamb, 48
Béarnaise, 32
Basic Fish, 74
Basic Lamb, 45
Bercy, 72
Bercy for Grilled
Meats, 81
Blue Cheese, 71
Cheddar-Sherry, 81
for Beef Steak, 26
Fresh Red Chili
Salsa, 84
Fresh Tomato and
Green Chile, 27
Fresh Tomato
Barbecue, 84
Guacamole, 27
Kebab, 22
Lemon-Butter, 39
Lime Basting, 48
Mexican for Beef, 27
Portugaise, 74
Potpourri, 83
Red Chili, 27
Rémoulade, 74
Shallot, 26
Simple Madeira, 30
Sweet-Sour Tomato
Barbecue, 84
Tomato, 74
Tomato Béarnaise, 25
Tomato-Soy, 58
Western, 84
Shellfish, see also Oyster,
Shrimp, etc.
How to Cook, 76
Kebabs, 78
Shrimp
Anchovy Appetizers, 79
Butterflied
Appetizers, 75
How to Cook, 76
Onigari Yaki, 78
Shellfish Kebabs, 78
Spicy Appetizers, 79
Skewer Combinations, 24
Skewer-Cooked
Beef
East Indian Saté, 23
Giant Lobster
Kebabs, 25
Ginger Teriyaki, 27
Hawaiian
Appetizers, 26
Oyster Appetizers, 21
Pakistani Kebabs, 24
Shish Koftesi, 22
Skewered Veal
Barbecue, 24
Skirts-Kebab, 21
Steak Kebabs, 29
Sweetbreads and
Steak Brochette, 22
Fish and Shellfish
Baluk Shish Kebab, 77
Beef-Oyster
Appetizers, 21

Fish and Shellfish
(cont'd.)
  Butterflied Shrimp
    Appetizers, 75
  Fish Kebabs
    Piraeus, 78
  Giant Beef-Lobster
    Kebabs, 25
  Onigari Yaki, 78
  Shellfish Kebabs, 78
  Shrimp and Anchovy
    Appetizers, 79
  Spicy Shrimp
    Appetizers, 79
Frank and Cheese
  Roll-ups, 91
Game, Ripple-Skewered
  Venison Steak
  Sandwiches, 61
Ginger-Buttered Fruit
  Kebabs, 86
Kebab Sauce, 22
Lamb
  Arni Souvlakia, 20
  in Onion Juice, 21
  Kebab Barg, 45
  Pakistani Kebabs, 24
  Rolls with Curry
    Honey Glaze, 23
  Russian Shashlik, 44
  Shish Koftesi, 22
  Sosaties with
    Fruit, 46
Mixed Vegetable
  Grill, 86
Mushrooms en
  Brochette,
  Flambé, 87
Parboiled Vegetables
  en Skewer, 88
Pineapple-Banana-
  Bacon Grill, 87
Pork
  Chinese
    Appetizers, 20
  Ham-Broiled Holiday
    Cherries, 91
  Indonesian Satés, 23
  Satés Bali, 50
Poultry
  Chicken Liver
    Kebabs, 25
  East Indian Saté, 23
  Indonesian Chicken
    Appetizers, 62
  Kamo No
    Koma-Giri, 70
  Pakistani Kebabs, 24
Skewer
  Combinations, 24
Toasted Bacon and
  Bread Pole, 91
Variety Meats
  Brochette de Rognons
    d'Agneau, 56
  Foie de Veau en
    Brochette, 56

Variety Meats (cont'd.)
  Liver 'n Bacon
    Grill, 57
  Mi'Laaf Mashivi, 56
  Peruvian
    Anticuchos, 57
  Zucchini-Tomato
    Kebabs, 86
Smoke-Cooked
  Beef
    Cumin Steak Strips
      and Cheese, 40
    Oyster-Topped
      Fillet, 41
    Rosemary Barbecued
      Sirloin, 39
    Smoked Sirloin
      Tip, 42
    Top Round Steak
      with Artichoke
      Hearts, 41
  Fish and Shellfish
    Oyster-Topped Beef
      Fillet, 41
    Salmon with Lemon
      Rice Stuffing, 72
    Smoked Fresh Salmon
      Fillet, 73
    Steaks with Bran, 77
  Lamb
    Garlic Leg, 49
    Smoked Leg, 48
  Pork
    Chinese Ribs, 55
    Hickory-Smoked Ham
      for a Crowd, 53
    Honey Glazed
      Ham, 55
    Loin with Prunes, 52
    Roast Loin on Melon
      Ring, 55
    Smoked Ribs in
      Barbecue Sauce, 54
  Poultry
    Buttery Cornish
      Hens, 66
    Duckling with Raisin
      Sauce, 70
    Smoke-Glazed
      Chicken, 64
    Smoked Chicken with
      Brandy Baste, 64
    Smoked Turkey, 68
    Smoky Turkey with
      Fruit Dressing, 67
    Surprised Squab, 69
    Teriyaki Turkey
      Roll, 68
    Turkey Parts in Blue
      Cheese Sauce, 71
  Variety Meats,
    Hickory-Smoked
      Tongue, 59
  Smoke Cooking, 11
    Aromatic Additives, 14
Spinach, Individual Meat
  Loaves, 58

Spit-Roasted
  Beef, Lazy Holiday
    Roast, 42
  Game, Venison Roast
    with Cinnamon
    Apples, 61
  Lamb
    Basque-
      Barbecued, 48
    Easy Leg, 48
    Lime-Basted Leg, 48
  Pork
    Garlic Spareribs, 54
    Rolled Leg, Hawaiian
      Style, 51
    Suckling Pig, 53
  Poultry
    Crisp-Roasted
      Goose, 71
    Duckling with Orange
      Baste, 68
    Pheasant with Cashew
      Stuffing, 71
    Spit-Roasted
      Chicken, 66
    Spit-Roasted
      Turkey, 67
    Spit-Roasted Wild
      Duck, 70
    Spit-Roasted Fruits
      and Vegetables, 87
  Variety Meats
    Broiled Tongue, 59
    Whole Liver with Salt
      Pork, 59
Spit Roasting, 14
  Balance Weight, 15
  Birds, 15
  Charts, 16, 17
  Direction of
    Rotation, 14
  Drip Pans, 14
  Pliers, 9
  Roasts, 15
  Spit Forks, 9
  Temperatures, 16, 17
  Times, 16, 17
Squab, Surprised, 69
Stuffing
  Fruit, 67
  Lemon Rice, 72
  Orange-Celery, 69
  Oyster, 31
Sweetbreads and Steak
  Brochette, 22

T

Teriyaki
  Baste, 63
  Marinade, 33
  Skirt Steaks, 35
  Steak Strips, 35
  Turkey Roll, 68
Tomato
  Béarnaise, 25
  Buttered, 88

Tomato (cont'd.)
  Fresh Barbecue
    Sauce, 84
  Ginger Baste with
    Variations, 85
  Sauce, 74
  Soy Sauce, 58
  Sweet-Sour Barbecue
    Sauce, 84
  Three-Way Relish, 82
  Zucchini Kebabs, 86
Tripe Strips in Butter, 56
Trout
  Butterflied, 77
  How to Bone, 77
Turkey
  Herb Butter Baste, 83
  Parts in Blue Cheese
    Sauce, 71
  Smoked, 68
  Smoky with Fruit
    Dressing, 67
  Spit-Roasted, 67
  Teriyaki Roll, 68
Turkish, Shish Koftesi, 22

V

Vegetable, see also
    Artichoke, Onion,
    Tomato, etc.
  Butter, 61
  Cooking in the
    Coals, 90
  Grilling in Foil, 89
  Ideas for Grilling, 87
  Mixed Grill, 86
  Parboiled en
    Skewer, 88
  Skewer
    Combinations, 24
  Spit-Roasted, 87
Venezuelan, Barbecued
  Pork, 50
Venison
  Grilled Steak, 60
  Ripple-Skewered Steak
    Sandwiches, 61
  Roast with Cinnamon
    Apples, 61
  Steak with Trio of
    Butters, 60
Volcanic Rock Coals, 7

Y

Yogurt
  Kebab Barg, 45
  Lela ka Kabab, 49
  Spicy Chicken, 62

Z

Zucchini-Tomato
  Kebabs, 86